"*Wrecked for God* is a work of ... culture shift from Christian w... of love and moving with the Holy Spirit has left many wondering what to do. Dianne Leman's book is a guide for many who are looking to make this vital shift!"

Danny Silk, president, Loving On Purpose;
author, *Keep Your Love On* and *Unpunishable*

"Dianne has unrelenting passion for, love for and pursuit of the Holy Spirit. This comes through loud and clear in *Wrecked for God*. With more than forty years building and leading a growing and vibrant church and fifty years as a lover of Jesus, she has valuable lessons to share with all who are thirsty for more."

Debby Wright, joint senior pastor, Trent Vineyard Nottingham;
joint national director, VCUKI

"How do we get wrecked for God? By living from the "I AM"—Jesus—who is the way, the truth and the life. Jesus is the finished work. He is the scandalous good news of the Gospel. The good news of the Gospel is not about finding ourselves but finding out that we have already been included in His finished work and we are hidden in Christ. It is not just Christ for us, but Christ in us. This revelation changes everything. . . . Di is a great teacher, communicator and seeker of truth. I love how she shares with honesty and transparency her own journey of discovery. Get ready to get wrecked for God and lose your religion—your self-effort to be good enough to be right with God—and all the fear and striving that come with that. Instead, be embraced by the faithfulness of Jesus, who is the glorious good news of the Gospel."

Brian Blount, author, *Putting Jesus on Display with Love and Power*; co–senior pastor, Crestwood Vineyard Church,
Oklahoma City, Oklahoma

"This is a beautifully written, heartfelt invitation to know Jesus. To really know Him. If you've wrestled with the disquieting sense that there must be more in your relationship with Him, you will find in *Wrecked for God* the words of a guide and a friend."

Kathryn Scott, senior pastor, Vineyard Anaheim

"*Wrecked for God* is a crash course in life lessons from a woman who pursues God passionately as much as anyone I know. Dianne's unique blend of teaching, life experience and prophetic conversation will open your eyes to how God has wrecked her, and you'll be wrecked as well!"

Putty Putman, founder, School of Kingdom Ministry

WRECKED
for
GOD

WRECKED

for

GOD

The Surprising Secret to

True Transformation

Dianne Leman

Chosen

a division of Baker Publishing Group

Minneapolis, Minnesota

© 2021 by Dianne Leman

Published by Chosen Books
11400 Hampshire Avenue South
Bloomington, Minnesota 55438
www.chosenbooks.com

Chosen Books is a division of
Baker Publishing Group, Grand Rapids, Michigan

Printed in the United States of America

Library of Congress Cataloging-in-Publication Data
Names: Leman, Dianne, author.
Title: Wrecked for God: the surprising secret to true transformation / Dianne Leman.
Description: Minneapolis, Minnesota: Chosen Books, a division of Baker Publishing Group, [2021]
Identifiers: LCCN 2020040217 | ISBN 9780800799960 (trade paperback) | ISBN 9780800762292 (casebound) | ISBN 9781493429875 (ebook)
Subjects: LCSH: Mystical union. | Christian life. | Spirituality—Christianity.
Classification: LCC BT767.7 .L45 2021 | DDC 234—dc23
LC record available at https://lccn.loc.gov/2020040217

Unless otherwise indicated, Scripture quotations are from The Holy Bible, English Standard Version® (ESV®), copyright © 2001 by Crossway, a publishing ministry of Good News Publishers. Used by permission. All rights reserved. ESV Text Edition: 2016

Scripture quotations labeled GNT are from the Good News Translation in Today's English Version-Second Edition. Copyright © 1992 by American Bible Society. Used by permission.

Scripture quotations labeled HCSB are from the Holman Christian Standard Bible®, copyright © 1999, 2000, 2002, 2003, 2009 by Holman Bible Publishers. Used by permission. Holman Christian Standard Bible®, Holman CSB®, and HCSB® are federally registered trademarks of Holman Bible Publishers.

Scripture quotations labeled KJV are from the King James Version of the Bible.

Scripture quotations labeled MSG are taken from THE MESSAGE, copyright © 1993, 2002, 2018 by Eugene H. Peterson. Used by permission of NavPress. All rights reserved. Represented by Tyndale House Publishers, Inc.

Scripture quotations labeled NASB are from the New American Standard Bible® (NASB), copyright © 1960, 1962, 1963, 1968, 1971, 1972, 1973, 1975, 1977, 1995 by The Lockman Foundation. Used by permission. www.Lockman.org

Scripture quotations labeled NIV are from THE HOLY BIBLE, NEW INTERNATIONAL VERSION®, NIV® Copyright © 1973, 1978, 1984, 2011 by Biblica, Inc.® Used by permission. All rights reserved worldwide.

Scripture quotations labeled NIV1984 are from the HOLY BIBLE, NEW INTERNATIONAL VERSION®. Copyright © 1973, 1978, 1984 Biblica. Used by permission of Zondervan. All rights reserved.

Scripture quotations labeled NLT are taken from the Holy Bible, New Living Translation, copyright © 1996, 2004, 2015 by Tyndale House Foundation. Used by permission of Tyndale House Publishers, Inc., Carol Stream, Illinois 60188. All rights reserved.

Scripture quotations labeled TLB are from The Living Bible, copyright © 1971. Used by permission of Tyndale House Publishers, Inc., Carol Stream, Illinois 60188. All rights reserved.

Scripture quotations labeled TPT are from The Passion Translation®. Copyright © 2017, 2018 by Passion & Fire Ministries, Inc. Used by permission. All rights reserved. ThePassionTranslation.com.

Scripture quotations marked YLT are from the Young's Literal Translation of the Bible.

In some cases, the identifying details of individuals have been changed to protect privacy.

Cover design by Darren Welch Design

21 22 23 24 25 26 27   7 6 5 4 3 2 1

green press
INITIATIVE

To my eighteen (and counting!) grandchildren,
I leave the priceless legacy of experiencing
God's best secret: Christ in you.

———————

And I pray that Christ will be more and more at home in your hearts, living within you as you trust in him. May your roots go down deep into the soil of God's marvelous love; and may you be able to feel and understand, as all God's children should, how long, how wide, how deep, and how high his love really is; and to experience this love for yourselves, though it is so great that you will never see the end of it or fully know or understand it. And so at last you will be filled up with God himself.

Ephesians 3:17–19 TLB

Contents

1. An Outright Scandal, an In-Sight Secret   33

SUBTITLE: God's secret is a hidden treasure, ready to be seen and too scandalous to ignore.

DILEMMA: What is this secret, and how do I discover it?

DESCRIPTION: While this secret has been revealed for thousands of years, it is now exploding in both academic and practical concern. Find out more!

2. Lost for Good, Found Forever   45

SUBTITLE: If you want to find Jesus, lose your religion—for good—and find true faith forever.

DILEMMA: I keep trying, but I can't seem to really find life in Jesus. Jesus, are You in me?

DESCRIPTION: Religion is the stumbling block that keeps us from finding Jesus and our true self. We can live free of fear, full of faith—in union with Him.

Foreword

Dianne Leman's new book, *Wrecked for God*, is the fruit of a lifetime of desiring to know God, follow God, obey God, celebrate and rest in God.

I first met Di and her husband, Happy, in 1984. They were the founders and lead pastors of a church of a few hundred at the time. The movement they were in was very legalistic and very religious. And, if I might say, oppressive of women. They left that movement and became part of the Vineyard movement in its early days. Today they pastor one of the largest Vineyard churches in the United States with several thousand who would call the Vineyard their home church. It is a great church full of love and mercy. Like any healthy organism, it grows, and the growth brings about change. I have witnessed many of these changes as I have interrelated with the Lemans.

Several years ago when I spoke at their church, I had the opportunity to hear Di speak on the Gospel. I could tell she was finding new insights and life in the message of grace. Now, several years later, Dianne has had time to allow the new insights to grow. *Wrecked for God* reflects these insights. The grace message in *Wrecked for God* has obviously brought life and freedom to Di. As I read the book, knowing her background, I can understand her excitement and the baggage she had been carrying around that she was able to lay aside. For this I, too, am excited.

There are many things I appreciate in *Wrecked for God*.

Di's research gives the book weight. I appreciate the quote from Bishop Charles Gore emphasizing our great need to connect the truth or insight of "Christ for us" with the truth or insight of "Christ in us." More emphasis has been given in the past to the former than to the latter, and I agree that both truths are important. Likewise I appreciate a parallel emphasis Di draws from the biblical scholar Constantine R. Campbell in his book *Paul and Union with Christ: An Exegetical and Theological Study*. The fact that Di did her homework on the concept of union with Christ is important to me.

Another insight Di highlights is the worldview that makes room for the supernatural. She draws on the concept of biblical scholar Paul Hiebert of the "excluded middle" in Western society, which has difficulty believing in angels, demons and the gifts of the Spirit. The churches of the West need to be awakened to the reality of this realm to become vibrant and to better relate to a postmodern context.

Di's stories in each chapter were able to sustain my interest throughout the book. As a storyteller myself, I appreciate the life they bring to the concepts she presents.

Likewise I appreciate her reading of Michael J. Gorman's *Participating in Christ: Explorations in Paul's Theology and Spirituality*. We need a stronger view of the transformative experience of being in Christ. She writes: "We are made righteous in our being. We are not just given some fake righteousness. We are made righteous. . . . This is more than a mere imputation. This is transformation." Many pages later Di comes back to this subject, quoting Gorman: "Transformation takes place in Christ by the working of the Spirit." Gorman goes on to write:

> Because this divine "force" is at work on us and within us, says Paul, we are being transformed into the glory and image of Christ. . . . "Be transformed by the renewal of your mind." . . . This call is in the passive voice because it is not merely our own effort that makes it happen. At the center of Paul's spirituality of participation and transformation is his notion of mutual indwelling, or reciprocal residence—that is, Christ in believers and believers in Christ.

I have full agreement with and excitement over this emphasis in Dianne's work.

She also quotes the book *Himself* by a key leader in the faith cure movement, A. B. Simpson, in regard to the emphasis on infusion: Christ in us. This major theme of the book I celebrate wholeheartedly. Two key sentences in chapter 6 encapsulate this theme: "Intimacy, not imitation. Passion, not performance."

Di discusses the relationship of obedience to intimacy. *Religion* seems to be a bad word and is seen in a very negative light—easily understood when I think of the kind of religion she experienced growing up, and even as a young woman. In trying to emphasize the finished work of Jesus as the basis for our standing apart from any works of our own, she pleads for relationship and intimacy, for the power of Christ in us to work through us.

This emphasis worried me for a while—that in rejecting faith plus works for salvation, she might have moved to faith without works, away from the Protestant emphasis of "faith that works." Our works have nothing to do with earning us our salvation; rather, once having come into salvation by grace, our love for the Savior is our motivation for good works. But Dianne seems to end up with the "faith that works" position of classic Protestantism and in line with Paul's position in Ephesians 2:8–10. As I read her book, I highlighted these statements: "Our relationship with God is at its best when we abide by His commands" and "We can be either too rigid with religion or too twisted with tolerance."

Her chapter 8 on ministry being messy is very helpful. I highlighted: "Ministry in union with Jesus is not a guarantee of one hundred percent success and zero percent failure. Far from it. But we can have one hundred percent freedom from fear of failure." In typical John Wimber language, she captures his heart, writing, "Everybody, not just trained, degreed ministers, gets to play or pray." How could we have Christ in us and not feel His leading to minister to others? This is an important chapter on ministry. When understood from the emphasis of the book on Christ living in us—He is our righteousness and makes us righteous—it is not difficult to understand that Christ in us by the Holy Spirit is the source of our love and passion, not only for the other members of the Trinity but for people.

Di's illustration of going to a large church in Southern California for the first time—how it confronted her religiousness and judgments—brought back great memories of visiting that same building, which did look more like a club than a church. Di was surprised by what people were wearing and the cigarettes being snuffed out as some of the people prepared to go into the service. There she and I both encountered an expression of church based on love and mercy. "Clearly these folks looked like they were more ready to party than to pray," she writes. "But this was a true church—a collection of sick in need of a doctor. . . . We had gathered at a church, but it was a church as Jesus intended—a hospital for sinners and not a museum for saints."

Wimber's influence on Di is clear in her paraphrase of one of his favorite sayings about ministry: "We like to say it is 'naturally supernatural' and not at all 'repulsively religious.'" Again she writes:

> This paradigm for ministry did not tell the sick that in order to be healed they must "meet God's conditions" or "get more faith" or "clean up" their messy lives. No, this paradigm lavished mercy, compassion and the unfailing love of God on all. Healing comes with compassion. Miracles follow mercy.

In the chapter "Messy Ministry," my favorite in the book, Di quotes Jesus:

> "Truly, truly, I say to you, the Son can do nothing of his own accord, but only what he sees the Father doing. For whatever the Father does, that the Son does likewise. For the Father loves the Son and shows him all that He himself is doing."
>
> John 5:19–20

Then she comments: "It seems crazy (yet encouraging) that Jesus could do nothing on His own. Jesus did only what the Father showed Him to do, and He was very aware that He could only do that." How are we to understand this statement in light of the kenotic passage of Philippians 2, in which Jesus "emptied himself"? The Bible teaches that Jesus was "the pioneer" of faith (Hebrews 12:2 NIV). Several translations add the pronoun *our* before *faith* and several do not. It is not present in the Greek text, though some assume it is implied. Also, Jesus did say we would be able to do what He did, and even greater things. The question is raised, then: How is this possible?

I believe the answer lies in what Di has emphasized—not just Christ for us, but Christ in us. Instead of seeing Jesus as our model for ministry, believing that in the incarnation He gave up His "omnis," including omnipotence, meaning He did what He did by the power of the Holy Spirit, as can we through the same Spirit—instead we recognize Jesus' two natures, divine and human. The argument is that His deity would not be deity if He did not have the power to work miracles.

Let us accept this as true: Not only did Jesus remain fully God and fully man, but He performed His miracles from His deity, as affirmed by the Third Council of Constantinople (AD 680–681). What does this mean for us? If our focus is on Christ dwelling in us, then we, too, have a new nature, a new presence—that of the Holy Spirit in us. As the incarnate second Person of the Trinity worked miracles not from His humanity but from His deity, so it is with us. By the power of the Trinity in us, God is able to work miracles through us. Not in our power, might, will or strength, but in the presence of the Father, Son and Holy Spirit, who have taken up residence in us through the new birth—the new creation, the indwelling Christ in us, "the hope of glory" (Colossians 1:27 NIV 1984). As Paul added, "To this end I labor, struggling with all his energy, which so powerfully works in me" (verse 29). When someone is healed through our prayers, it is not we who healed the person, but God in us who healed him or her—His energy which "so powerfully works" in us.

Because of the cross, the New Covenant has been enacted and the Spirit has been poured out upon us. Our new birth is of the Spirit and from above. This new birth is not just a new relationship to God, not a fictitious righteousness, but a true righteousness made possible by the triune God, who has come into us. We are no longer what we were prior to our regeneration by the Spirit. There is more to us. We, too, have God in us, making it possible for miracles to happen by the will and power of God in us.

Jesus is our model still. Irenaeus, bishop of Lyon (AD 130–202), said, "He became what we are that we might become what He is." Athanasius (c. AD 296 or 298–373), another great leader in the early Church, said, "He became man so that we might become god." We must understand Athanasius's statement in light of 2 Peter 1:3–4 (NIV1984):

> His divine power has given us everything we need for life and godliness through our knowledge of him who called us by his own glory and goodness. Through these he has given us his very great and precious promises, so that through them you may participate in the divine nature and escape the corruption in the world caused by evil desires.

Because of Christ in us, we can participate in the divine nature. We in our humanity must also say, "I can do nothing of myself." What I do of a miraculous nature is the work of the Spirit of God within me, not my doing. I can heal no one; God is the healer. Christ in me is the hope I have of seeing the glory of God worked through me.

Another of my favorite chapters in Dianne's book is "Powerful, Not Pagan," on the subject of prayer. I like Di's take on not just "practicing the presence" (a quote from Brother Lawrence) but "participating in His presence." This moves from imitating

Him to participating in the union we have with Christ. I do think Brother Lawrence might have agreed with Di—that the only way to truly practice the presence is by participating in the presence. Hence, practicing the presence of Jesus is participating in His presence in me.

Her teaching from John 15 about abiding in Jesus as the vine and about His words abiding in us has great impact on our ability to ask in prayer. She writes that it was medically impossible for her to have children, but God used the words of Scripture to give her faith and five children born naturally. "God answers prayer according to His will," she writes, "and we can know His will from His Word." Her honesty in this section about her personal life was refreshing. And she has many good insights on prayer: the value of the Holy Spirit in prayer; having a prayer language; prayer as communication (so needed for a healthy relationship); prayer as worship, warfare and rejoicing; and how to pray in the midst of crisis—with persistence.

In the last chapter, I was grateful to see Di's balance in acknowledging our sins and shortcomings and our need to have the Father prune these from our lives. She knows the lack of wisdom in some who embraced such a strong grace message that they did not deal with the dead branches, the sins, and as a result did not acknowledge sin in their lives, thinking this would deny the truth of the success of the cross, the new creation and their identity as righteous saints. Di notes that "this denial thwarted the work of transformation that the Spirit wanted to do in order to make Christ's image more visible and vibrant in their lives." For me this brings balance to the book, leaving a place for dealing with our sins in a relationship of grace. While I am forgiven already, it is still important to remove anything that would grieve the Lover of my soul by saying, "I'm sorry," and thanking Him for His forgiveness.

Another of the teachings I appreciate a great deal is that Di makes clear she does not believe in universalism. The message of grace does not mean grace for all, but grace for those who believe. She marks a difference between herself and grace teachers who have ended up in universalism.

In summary, I take away as a primary emphasis that grace is not a legal fiction, nor is righteousness fictitious. Instead grace is strongly related to the reality of Christ living in us, who is Himself the source of grace. Grace is the power to live victoriously. Christ in us is the hope of glory and the power of God working in and through us. Grace is more than unmerited mercy and forgiveness; it is also undeserved divine enablement and empowerment.

Randy Clark, D.D., D.Min., Th.D., M.Div., B.S., religious studies overseer, Apostolic Network of Global Awakening; president, Global Awakening Theological Seminary

Acknowledgments

Nowadays it is rare to receive a thank-you note in the mail. But I am old fashioned and still love to have my gift giving acknowledged with a few written words of thanks. (Hint to all children and grandchildren.) Hence, I want not only to acknowledge but also to thank with all my heart those who have given me their gifts that helped to make *Wrecked* a beautiful wreck.

Thank You, Holy Spirit, for coming through on Your promise to write every word in union with me.

Thank you, Randy Clark, for honoring me with your theological expertise and most of all your friendship.

Thank you, The Vineyard Church of Central Illinois, for giving me the privilege of preaching, pastoring and learning these truths while making lots of mistakes.

Thank you, Ramona, Shelly, Valencia and Rosie, for your fierce but friendly feedback.

Thank you, Jane Campbell, for helping me believe in God's writing gift to me and giving me a chance with Chosen Books.

Thank you, Christy Callahan, for being an accurate, talented, but most of all, fun-loving editor whose humor healed any of my humiliating editorial errors.

Thank you, Happy Leman, for prodding me—in true marital devotion and love—never to give up even when I wanted to (many, many times).

And—"Thanks be to God! For in union with Christ we are always led by God as prisoners in Christ's victory procession. God uses us to make the knowledge about Christ spread everywhere like a sweet fragrance" (2 Corinthians 2:14 GNT).

Introduction

God's Best Secret

God loves secrets. No wonder—most of us do, too. We are made in His image, true children of our Father. He has kept some of His secrets hidden for many years, but now He has chosen to make them known. These are things the prophets of old clamored to know more about. They sensed these secrets were sensational. They were right. But they were told their messages were not for them. God's secrets, including His very best one, were for a people to come. We are those people. Do we realize how fortunate we are? Even the angels "would have given anything to be in on this" (1 Peter 1:12 MSG). They are now watching how we live out such astounding truths. Let's not disappoint them.

The surprising secret to the Christian life, kept hidden for generations but now revealed, is not more prayer, more study, more giving, more surrender, more sacrifice. This secret is not more of me or more of you doing anything more. No, the secret to the Christian life is more exciting and far less exhausting than that. What is this secret to true transformation? This secret is

Christ in me, Christ in you. Not *more* of Him, but *all* of Him—the fullness of Christ in each of us, all of us.

This secret was first revealed by Paul:

> There is a divine mystery—a secret surprise that has been concealed from the world for generations, but now it's being revealed, unfolded and manifested for every holy believer to experience. Living within you is the Christ who floods you with the expectation of glory! This mystery of Christ, embedded within us, becomes a heavenly treasure chest of hope filled with the riches of glory for his people, and God wants everyone to know it!
>
> Colossians 1:26–27 TPT

God wants everyone to know this: Living within you, within me, is the Christ. He is embedded within us. And this, my friend, is the secret above all secrets, kept hidden for centuries but now made known. The triune nature of God is complex for sure, but Paul clarifies this truth for us:

> You, however, are not in the flesh but in the Spirit, if in fact the Spirit of God dwells in you. Anyone who does not have the Spirit of Christ does not belong to him. But if Christ is in you, although the body is dead because of sin, the Spirit is life because of righteousness.
>
> Romans 8:9–10

All who have ears to hear can know God's secret and enjoy a transformed life. That is what we are yearning for, after all. That is why we buy books that promise life-changing secrets, right? I have been a sucker for such books. I have wanted to read the miracle secret—to losing weight, making money, raising successful children, enjoying a happy marriage, praying powerful prayers, healing the sick, loving God and loving others. I have paid plenty to read others' secrets. Plenty of money. Plenty of time. The reading is the easy part. We like easy. We want the promised results without the prescribed effort.

With God's secret, there is no instant transformation, although we have peace and joy every day. This is not easy, but it is simple. Your whole life can be wrecked for good. Your whole life can be wrecked for God. And you will experience true transformation.

Wrecked for good and for God. True transformation.

That is what we want, too.

Less anger. More patience. Greater joy. No depression. Slower pace. Richer relationships. Better sleep. Genuine faith. Deeper love. We do not want to stay the same. We ache for change. We want it—*fast, free and fun filled, please.* We have neither the time nor the tenacity to wait. We buy books, plans and pills that promise prompt and painless transformation. And we despair once again when we wake unchanged.

I hope to change that, no pun intended. Not by my great wisdom or power, but by sharing with you the surprising secret to true transformation that brings real change and is for everyone. It is not an overnight overhaul. It will take some time and lots of trust. But you will delight in the new you. Your hope for change will no longer be deferred, and the sickness in your soul will be made well. That is His promise, and He is ready to provide.

Did you know this desire for change—for a healthier, more satisfying life—is a God-given desire? This is because He has much more for each of us, and He implants within us "the passion to do what pleases him" (Philippians 2:13 TPT). Perhaps this is why you have continued to wonder—wonder if there was more to the Good News than you have heard preached. More to knowing Jesus than you have experienced. Maybe you compared your faith to those Facebook folks who only show the "highlight reel" and tend to fan our feeble faith into flames of failure.

Perhaps you have been tempted to give up on your faith—a faith that feels more like a veneer to cover your disappointment and disillusionment rather than one that strengthens you through the storms. I am embarrassed to admit that was my story. I was frustrated with my life as a disciple of Jesus. I was grateful for everything He had done, but not satisfied. I am thankful I was compelled to run toward God, not away, and to search for His wisdom and help. Over time (I know, I wish it were quick), He answered me with extravagant wisdom and Holy Spirit help. I wanted a forever faith, and that is exactly what I have discovered: the faith of the Son of God, who loved me and gave His life for me and moved right inside me to anchor me for eternity.

Why had I made the Christian life so hard, exhausting, unenjoyable? Why had I made it self-centered when God had made it Savior centered? God made it possible for us to have "everything in abundance, more than you expect—life in its fullness until you overflow!" (John 10:10 TPT). But we live in a tumultuous time. Megachurch pastors, who seemed to have all the ministry success others craved, in truth, were tormented enough to take their own lives. Scores of desperate Christians, old and young, have deconstructed their faith and then failed to reconstruct a belief that breathed life into their dying souls. Unprecedented numbers of prominent Christians are leaving the faith, writing and speaking about their angst and provoking a dangerous doubt among the faithful.

Better to wrestle, doubt, even deconstruct than to pretend all is well when your spirit is sick and your thirsty soul cries out for living water. But will you stop and take a drink? Will you read these pages and ask the Holy Spirit to reignite a faith in Jesus so "rivers of living water will burst out from within you" (John 7:38 TPT)? I pray that *Wrecked for God* will play a part, even if just a small part, in God's plan to help you grow into the fullness of Jesus Christ. I pray you, too, will discover God's surprising secret for all, a secret that brings true transformation.

This is the book I wanted to read over thirty years ago when I first heard a teacher share God's surprising secret, His best secret. Now I am the writer, and you are the reader. My heart burns with excitement, and I pray yours will, too, as you learn and live the astounding truth of this secret. God saved the best for last. God's best secret is no longer a secret. That is great news for us. This is not some Gnostic babble where only a few who are super spiritual and uberqualified can partake. God's best secret is for everyone. And that includes you and me.

Am I an expert at living in union with God?

No way.

Have I learned some valuable lessons?

Yes, and I know the Holy Spirit will personalize them for you. These are lessons that apply to everyone, everywhere—which gives me great confidence they are lessons from God and not from me.

I have attempted to write this book several times. I felt compelled to support every idea and experience with a Bible verse because union with Christ is controversial and often misunderstood. I forced verses to prove my points, and this cramped my style and sounded too preachy and pretty pathetic. I did not want to read what I wrote, and I was pretty sure you would not want to either.

"God, do You want me to write this book, or should I just forget it, not force it?" I moaned to Jesus.

I moaned to my daughter. I moaned to my husband.

I am thankful that despite my discouragement, my passion persisted. I found a soul mate in Paul and his words to the Ephesians: "My passion is to enlighten every person to this divine mystery. It was hidden for ages past until now, and kept a secret in the heart of God, the Creator of all" (Ephesians 3:9 TPT).

I was consumed with telling the world God's best secret, even if I struggled and no one wanted to read. And then I heard Jesus say the obvious to me, *Why don't we write this book together?*

Duh. This is a book on Jesus living in me, and I was trying to write it on my own. No wonder it stunk. It is not as if I did not ask the Holy Spirit for help in all my attempts to write. I did. But, as it is with so much of life, I asked for divine help and then proceeded to do it myself, thank you very much. I tried to write without listening to Him and without partnering with Him. Bingo! That is the core message of this entire book.

My life is first and foremost about Him. Jesus is the hero. He lives in me. I live in Him. We are one. But in my wretched writing attempts, I was making it about me. I kept doing this alone. That would stop. We would write this book together. I would hear His heart and wisdom on how to share what He has worked in my life for a long time. The focus would be on Jesus, as it should be. Jesus is for everyone. Union with Jesus is for everyone.

But a life of union with Christ is not automatic. While it is already accomplished—thanks to the finished work of Jesus—we have a hard time learning and living the lesson that apart from Him, we can do nothing. And that nothing includes writing a book about this union we share. I am always in a hurry; God, not so much. I want to be efficient and quick. God seems satisfied with slow and messy. But His results are far superior.

We embark on a journey of living daily, moment by moment, in the reality of His unfailing love with no fear. We have much to learn about this new life with God inside. There is no automatic, instant transformation, but there is His constant presence. And His presence brings true transformation. We can trust His timing. That is not always easy, especially for an impatient one like me. We can trust His tenderness and His toughness. I like the tender, but the tough has been, well, tough. But through it all, I know we can trust Christ in us, loving us, changing us. He, in us, is the secret to true transformation. We are the actual home of God. We cannot live the Christian life. Only Christ can live the Christ life, and He longs to do it in and through each of us and our unique personalities.

Are you ready to be wrecked for good? Do you long for true transformation? Then read on and begin to live a life in union with Jesus. Begin to enjoy the deep satisfaction of knowing you are loved and never need to be lonely or afraid again. Embrace the secret of Christ in you, now and forever. This is the surprising secret to true transformation. Get ready to be wrecked for God. He is drawing you, and I am cheering you on.

An Outright Scandal, an In-Sight Secret

God's secret is a hidden treasure, ready to be seen and too scandalous to ignore.

WHAT IS THIS SECRET, AND HOW DO I DISCOVER IT?

In 2014 a Northern California couple spotted an old can sticking out of the ground on their property. They had never seen this, although they had walked this same trail many times. The man managed to remove the can from the ground, loosen the rusty lid and peer inside. He was shocked to discover it was filled to the brim with gold coins. They eventually uncovered a total of eight cans with over 1,400 rare U.S. gold coins. Despite being buried for over a hundred years, many of the coins were preserved in pristine condition. This was the biggest find in U.S. history—$10 million—and it was there all along, buried on their property. That treasure brought transformation to their lives.[1]

Jesus, the ultimate treasure, is buried in each of us, and it is time to discover this hidden gift, far more valuable than any amount of gold. I join with Paul's prayer:

> I am contending for you that your hearts will be wrapped in the comfort of heaven and woven together into love's fabric. This will give you access to all the riches of God as you experience the revelation of God's great mystery—Christ. For our spiritual wealth is in him, like hidden treasure waiting to be discovered—heaven's wisdom and endless riches of revelation knowledge.
>
> Colossians 2:2–3 TPT

Treasure for transformation. We can look forward to a transformed life as chosen children of God, filled with all the riches of Christ. God cares deeply about everything in our lives: our battle with depression, the heartache of rebellious kids, the disappointment of unanswered prayer, struggles with our weight, the stress of unpaid bills, the fear of the cancer diagnosis and the many temptations we strive to overcome. He also wants us to truly enjoy the wonder of our newborn, the comfort of the cardinal's song, the excitement of the soccer match, the beauty of the springtime dogwood, the rich aroma of a freshly brewed latte (and the sugary delight of the donut), plus the daily peace all of us yearn for.

God cares about every detail of our lives, even the number of hairs on our head, which changes daily for many of us. He, God Almighty, became a human being. He is one of us. He is all God, too. "The Word became flesh and blood, and moved into the neighborhood" (John 1:14 MSG). He not only moved into the neighborhood, He moved right on inside us. That move means

Jesus "gets" us—the good, the bad and the ugly—and loves to bring transformation to all of life.

While you can study and discuss this secret, you cannot experience the depths of it without some time and lots of humility. That means you get good at admitting, "I don't know" and "I can't" or "I was wrong." God's best secret is the answer, resulting in a transformed life. Christ in me is not just a "faith fact." This is a truth that sets you free.

Get ready to discover this most glorious hidden treasure—Christ in you. Is there anything more exhilarating than finding a treasure, especially a treasure that was there all along and you did not know it?

A Transformed Life—Consumed with Christ

Life moves at a frantic pace. We live in a fast-food, drive-through world. Our phones are buzzing, our computers calling. It is easy to forget that fundamental truth Jesus made clear—apart from Him, we can do nothing (see John 15:5). No thing, as in nothing at all. We need help, and that is precisely what our union with Jesus provides. We live with a Helper, the Holy Spirit Himself, right inside of us. But living with another Person, especially when He is inside of you and He is God, brings challenges. The relationship Jesus offers to each of us is the very same union He shares with the Father and Holy Spirit. Even if this is hard to digest, it is not farcical nor heretical. Our union with Christ is one hundred percent true and one hundred percent transformative.

Let me assure you—embracing this truth will be intriguing and invigorating, but also inexplicable. But seeking God's best secret is worth our time and our trust. In the process, we will be wrecked—and *wrecked* is a positive word in the 21st century.

Despite all the confusion, contradiction and craziness that life brings, we can be wrecked for good and for God. We can learn to love and live God's best secret. We can be transformed in union with Him. This is a journey filled with puzzling paradoxes, with some real pain, but plenty of pleasure, too. It is a bumpy, yet beautiful journey. Yet we are safe. We are loved. We are cared for. We are already in union with Jesus Christ. He lives in us. This is what His finished work on the cross and glorious resurrection made possible. Right before He went to the cross, Jesus reminded us: "I will not leave you as orphans; I will come to you. Yet a little while and the world will see me no more, but you will see me. Because I live, you also will live. In that day you will know that I am in my Father, and you in me, and I in you" (John 14:18–20).

He is not going anywhere. He lives in us. We are not trying to get to Him or be perfect enough to warrant His moving inside of us. He already lives in us. Our union, our oneness with Jesus, is not our destination; it is our starting point. This is where many have been tripped up and stalled throughout church history. Our union with Christ has been taught as the destination, the goal of the Christian life. Such wrong teaching has resulted in much frustration, disappointment, exhaustion and even abandonment of the faith. How tragic. We do not ascend level after level until we achieve union with Christ. We are already in union with Christ. We are not looking for a way to be in union with Him. He is the Way. He made it possible for Himself to move inside of us. He washed us clean, made us new, by His shed blood and broken body and now shares His resurrected life with each of us.

Jesus chose Paul, the great Hebrew scholar, to relate through pen and preaching the fuller revelation of Christ in us. It pleased God to reveal this secret, His Son, in Paul (see Galatians 1:16).

The transformation of Saul, who was called Paul as well (see Acts 13:9), was undeniable. He went from killing followers of the Way—a cold-blooded murderer—to living with the Way inside of him. No doubt this is one of the greatest transformations in all of history. Paul took seriously the commission to tell the world about this secret, God's best secret, Christ in us. Paul was obsessed with this reality and wanted everyone to know. He agonized as a woman in labor until his hearers experienced the fullness of Christ in them (see Galatians 4:19). That is a serious obsession. I have labored through five births, and I can feel Paul's intense desire for us to get this. I want in. Or should I say, I want to experience the fullness of Christ in me. Jesus is "the way, the truth, and the life" (John 14:6 NLT). This is more than a great Bible verse. Jesus is all of the above—in us. The hard work is done. Let the fun begin.

An In-Sight Secret, a Big Change

An undeniable, dominant theme in all the Pauline epistles is this close and indissoluble union we have with the Lord Jesus Christ. Paul sums up our union with the short phrase "in Christ," which appears in different ways over two hundred times in his writings (in contrast, the word *Christian* appears only three times in the entire Bible).[2] I think the Holy Spirit is trying to make a point, a once-sharp point that man-made religions have managed to minimize over the centuries. "In Christ" is much more than an oft-repeated, but easily overlooked, Bible truth or a phrase to be memorized and mounted on our bathroom mirror. This "in Christ" revelation is God's best secret that empowers us to live fully human, fully alive in the finished work of Jesus. We no longer have to struggle, strive and suffocate under our own works.

It is worth unraveling this mystery. *Mystery* is a great description of how God's secrets unfold. In fact, the word *mystery* is a synonym for the word *secret* as used in the New Testament.[3] Our union with Christ is a mystery in many ways. Like any good mystery, you need to be prepared for lots of twists, turns and surprises and be willing to embrace some radical revelation. That is what makes a story worth reading, right? In the same way, this is what makes a life worth living—life filled with surprises and challenges that keep us dependent on the One who lives inside us.

The Holy Spirit has been unraveling this mystery, revealing this secret for several thousands of years, but we have not always had ears that hear. And that is downright scandalous. In 1921 Charles Gore, Bishop of Oxford and one of the most influential Anglican theologians of his time, said, "Theology's failure to unite 'Christ *for* us' with the 'Christ *in* us' is nothing less than an outright scandal."[4] An outright scandal and an insight secret. Christ in us. The secret is not just Christ, or Christ for us, but Christ in us. This is a huge difference—more than the simple preposition *in* conveys. Let that sink in.

When I first learned this secret, I was captivated. I knew I wanted to experience this mystery, this secret, this almost impossible dream of my union, my oneness with Christ. I searched for someone to give me the steps to living with God inside me. After all, that is pretty preposterous. God in me? But this is the absolute mystery and majesty of the glorious Good News. I hungered for a clearer, deeper revelation of this Good News, this mystical union with Christ. I prayed daily that Jesus would be "more and more at home" in my heart, living inside of me as I trusted Him (Ephesians 3:17 TLB).

While I encountered plenty of Catholic mystics, Puritan preachers, Holiness writers, devout missionaries and contemporary teachers who helped guide me in my quest, I was still frustrated. My life did not match what Scripture revealed was possible—living in a loving union with Jesus, complete with abundant fruit, answered prayers, strength in suffering and signs and wonders to boot. I experienced God's goodness, grace and faithfulness in many ways. I was and am forever grateful. But I was not content to live a life that did not more fully reflect Christ in me. I tried hard to make "me" decrease and make Jesus increase, although I was pretty clueless about what that meant. I worked hard to crucify (kill off) any part of "me" that was misbehaving. When that failed, I focused on finding a more positive "me"—my best self for Jesus. I discovered ways to improve my life, embrace my destiny, grow strong in character and, of course, love God and love people more. But I was not satisfied.

I listened to an intriguing interview of a man whose life had been transformed by this secret of union with Christ. I was eager to purchase his book since he did not have the chance to tell his whole story in a thirty-minute podcast. What were the obstacles he encountered? What were the aha moments he experienced, the unexpected joys, the confusing dilemmas and the ultimate victories of learning to live in union with Christ? Despite its length of several hundred pages, this man's book—one filled with Scriptures, prescriptions for lifestyle changes and accounts of God's amazing grace in his own life—was a huge disappointment. Where were the tales of temptation, the stories of struggle, the accounts of anxiety as he navigated the reality of living in union with Jesus? It is an outright scandal and an in-sight secret that we live out in real life. But how?

Then, things began to change. This was the change I desperately wanted. I discovered this journey was not all about me—my identity, my destiny, my maturity, my ministry, my transformation. No, this journey has been about Jesus, not me. Yes, I know I probably said all along that my quest was about Jesus. But try as I might, Jesus Christ's magnificence seemed to elude me.

Not anymore.

Now I am delighted to share with you Christ in me, plus all the lessons He has taught me about our union, our oneness, which is God's best secret. I can sum up these lessons in one statement: Jesus has gotten bigger, better and more beautiful than I ever dared to dream or imagine. And this has wrecked me for good and for God. A surprising and life-changing thing happened along the way. I experienced that "more than we would ever dare to ask or even dream of" dynamic that Paul wrote about and we all quote and pray (Ephesians 3:20 TLB). Never did I imagine that as Jesus Christ got bigger, better and more beautiful to me, I would begin to see myself as He saw me—bigger, better and more beautiful than I ever imagined I could be. That is how true transformation happened.

I was undone. I was wrecked for God.

I knew I wanted to tell others about this secret that puts into perspective our failures and frustrations with faith. And I received my confirmation to write on this from God in an unusual but convincing way. I always peruse the Book of the Year awards in various publications and was intrigued when I saw that *Christianity Today* magazine's 2014 selection in Biblical Studies was *Paul and Union with Christ: An Exegetical and Theological Study* by Constantine Campbell.[5] According to its description on Amazon, this book

> fills the gap for biblical scholars, theologians, and pastors pondering and debating the meaning of union with Christ. Follow-

ing a selective survey of the scholarly work on union with Christ through the twentieth century to the present day, Greek scholar Constantine Campbell carefully examines every occurrence of the phrases 'in Christ,' 'with Christ,' 'through Christ,' 'into Christ,' and other related expressions, exegeting each passage in context and taking into account the unique lexical contribution of each Greek preposition.[6]

Immediately I was gripped with a Holy Spirit urgency to read this 480-page scholarly tome. Although I struggled to get through it (and skipped a few pages), I knew it was God when I read Campbell's directive:

Finally, a future direction stemming from this study could be the exploration of the pastoral and devotional implications of union with Christ. This could take place on a more popular— rather than academic—level, for the sake of distilling important theological observations to be of widespread benefit to the life of the church. It ought to be clear that union with Christ offers a wealth of pastoral and devotional potential and should be extolled from every pulpit and basic to every believer.[7]

I wrote in the margin, *This is my assignment from the Holy Spirit*.

I want to be one of the voices that takes this core Gospel truth of union with Christ and extols practical, pastoral and devotional implications for the ordinary person. Why was this so significant to me? I am not a Greek scholar. I am not a biblical academician. The letters after my name are M.Ed., not M.Div. I do not pretend to be an exegetical or theological whiz.[8] But I love the Bible, and I love Jesus.

41

The Divine Nature in Us

Jesus said His work was "finished" (John 19:30), and we get to partake now of His divine nature and live in union with Him. But while this happens instantaneously and completely, we each need to learn to live in the glorious truth. That is a journey. That is true transformation. Not just mental assimilation of incredible revelation and information, as important as that knowledge is. This growth takes time, yet the truth remains: We are already in union with Christ. We are not trying to work our way into union, but we are working out our salvation, our union, with Him. We are one with God!

I can hear the protests and questions now.

Dianne, if we are one with God, are you saying we become God?

The short answer is no. But we are partakers of the divine nature, and that changes everything (see 2 Peter 1:4).

If I'm in union with Christ, do I just disappear and Jesus takes over?

No. You stay you, the real you, but without sin and selfishness. Life in union with Christ is so much better. It is easy to make a mess of our lives when we attempt to tackle life on our own. We are especially captive to old mindsets that result in temporarily satisfying but inferior lifestyles. Our Christian life can quickly become frustrating and boring. We encounter and endure suffering that shakes our faith and steals our peace. Our love for Jesus grows lukewarm. When this happens, we plummet into dark sin and shame.

God has jerked me back to safety when I have been spiraling down into confusion or tottering on the cliff of spiritual suicide. I have heard Him say: *It can be wrong to be right; beware the*

Bible; *stop imitating Jesus*; *come out of the grave*; *get drunk daily*; *don't sin less*; *lose your religion, not your faith*—to name just a few. And I will explore all of these in this book. At first, these statements sound dangerous, wrong or downright confusing. I have a history of being skeptical and afraid of being deceived. The Holy Spirit unearthed my faulty beliefs and twisted versions of Christianity that trapped me and kept me from seeing Jesus and myself. Religion without revelation and relationship is ruthless and fruitless.

My Father wanted me to stop and listen, to see things from a different angle. He is such a good, good Father. He wants to rearrange our thinking so we can embrace the full life He offers. We are God's home. I am still me. You are still you. We do not become Christian clones or religious robots. We do come alive. We become who He designed us to be with all our gifts, calling and destiny. We see ourselves as He sees us—bigger, better and far more beautiful than we ever imagined.

I thought of this as I watched my beautiful newborn granddaughter Molly. She smiled, cooed and flailed her tiny arms while she lay on the pink quilted blanket. She cannot sit, walk, talk, dress or feed herself. She is just one month old. But she has all the unique DNA she will ever need to become a full-grown woman someday. She cannot try to add to that DNA; she can only continue to be transformed day by day, month by month, year by year. In the same way, we have divine DNA. We have Christ in us. But like Molly, we are newborns who need to depend on Him to grow into the fullness of who He designed us to be.

Let's take off our religious robes and picture Christ in us. Allow yourself to dance a jig or a waltz, or maybe even hip-hop with Him. I can see Him smiling now. He so loves to live in union with us.

43

Why Does This Matter?

"We are like common clay jars that carry this glorious treasure within, so that the extraordinary overflow of power will be seen as God's, not ours" (2 Corinthians 4:7 TPT). We have this treasure hidden in our clay pots—pots that are cracked by the chaos of life. We can choose to live in that chaos or in Christ. We can choose to be crushed or to overflow with His power and light.

We know the secret. You can find the real you, the beautiful you that God our Father destined for you to be before you were even in your mother's womb (see Jeremiah 1:5). Christ is not going anywhere. He has made His home in us. Will we welcome Him? Will we partner with His Spirit as He brings true transformation?

What Can I Do Right Now?

Grab a cup of coffee, or some tea or a glass of sauvignon blanc, and settle in as we hunker down with the Holy Spirit and invite Him to do what He does best: unravel the mystery of Christ in us.

Father, open the eyes of my heart to see and experience Your secret of Christ in me.

2

Lost for Good, Found Forever

If you want to find Jesus, lose your religion—
for good—and find true faith forever.

I KEEP TRYING, BUT I CAN'T SEEM TO REALLY FIND LIFE
IN JESUS. JESUS, ARE YOU IN ME?

My period was late. I was petrified that I was pregnant. I was
a smart college-bound high school junior. It was 1968, and
even if abortion were legal, it would never be an option in my
world. But a baby would ruin my life. Worse, a teenage pregnancy would ruin my parents' life, a life firmly entrenched in
a religion that would drown them in shame if an unmarried
daughter was pregnant. I had no comfort of family or faith. Our
family's religion demanded a young girl surrender all dating,
sports, music, drama, jewelry, makeup and movies in order to
be acceptable to God. All women were commanded to embrace

45

this ascetic lifestyle along with mortifying, modest dresses and black veils to cover their exposed heads. Women must display their submission to God and men. Did I mention it was a sin to have fun and a shame to feel fervor of any kind except for this "faith"? At least I had the choice to say "No, thank you" to church membership (and the above misery). I could still attend Sunday services as a nonmember and did every week out of obedient respect for my parents. But I knew deep in my heart that until I repented of my sinful, shameful self, I was unacceptable to them, to the church and, worse, to God.

With a looming pregnancy, I was alone in my cage of fear and consumed with finding a way out. My fear compelled me to seek solace in someone or something more powerful or more promising. I could choose a disastrous dalliance with drugs or "by chance" choose a more helpful path. Thankfully, I turned to the Young Life club at my school, a group of teens and adult leaders who, to the horror of my parents, claimed to be Christians but were quite free and fun loving in their practice of faith. Now, over fifty years later, I know that was the love of the Father, who directed me there. But at the time, it was a random, somewhat rebellious and desperate step to deal with my fear and find peace.

I was at a Wednesday night Young Life gathering when I was handed a book, *How to Be a Christian Without Being Religious* by Fritz Ridenour. (Thank you, Amazon, for helping me recall the author; thank You, God, for whispering that this book may change someone else's life, too.) The club leader thought this author addressed some of my fears and questions about faith. I agreed to take a look. I certainly did not know that the loving God of the universe was defining my destiny with this book. While it would be five more years before I became a Christian, the Spirit was assigning my life's quest via this little book—how to be a Christian without being religious.

This was a dangerous quest for a girl who was expected to bow to the strict, oppressive religion of her mother, grandmother and great-grandmother before her. This was an unlikely destiny for a girl who dreamed of being a famous actress and stunning the world with her beauty and brains. This quest, unlike those resolved in a 45-minute TV episode, took me quite a few years to fully embrace. But over time, Jesus has become much bigger than any fear and far better and more beautiful than any man-made religion or Dianne-designed dream. I have learned how to be a Christian, a real lover of Jesus, without being religious. I had to lose that religion for good and find true faith, the faith of the Son of God, who loved me and gave His life for me (see Galatians 2:20). This Jesus, who paid with His body and blood for me, Dianne Marie, does not demand that I cover my head in submission to men or cower in shame for my passion. Daily He showers my head with unfailing love and embraces me with sheer delight. And He longs to do the same for you.

By the way . . . my fear of a ruinous, unwanted pregnancy was unfounded. But this was not for the usual reason that somehow miraculously I had escaped the consequences of a careless night of passion. My well-meaning but ill-advised and deeply religious mother had shared her version of the "birds and bees" talk with me with a special emphasis on "you know you can get pregnant without ever having sex." This was a scare tactic spoken in love by a generation of moms to their daughters on the cusp of a dangerous sexual revolution. With naiveté, I had surmised that the recent passionate making out with my boyfriend had somehow impregnated me. A flood of relief accompanied the delayed, but unmistakable, monthly flood of menses. My fear was gone. For then. But fear has a way of finding a way back into our lives to torment our souls and crush our faith. And religion is the villain who wields this weapon of war against us, robbing us of true trust.

Repulsive, Fear-Based Religion

"I've had it with you," the angry man seethed. "You're no better than a bunch of snakes, reptilian sneaks! You think you look good—all fancy and fixed up—but I know what you are really like on the inside—maggot-infested flesh. You're hopeless, arrogant, stupid frauds. You might fool yourselves, but you don't fool me. It's over for you."

This is a scathing rebuke, an accusation that cuts through carefully crafted facades and exposes the real rot inside. This is Jesus speaking.[1] Jesus is downright mad. Who provoked Jesus' anger? Was it the sleazy streetwalkers who prostituted their bodies and dressed in gaudy finery? Was it those corrupt business folks who swindled the poor while pretending to protect the law? Was it the cruel Roman soldiers, dressed in royal regalia, who mercilessly oppressed God's people? None of those folks sent Jesus into such a rage, despite the obvious sinfulness of their behavior. Jesus' anger was directed at the self-righteous, religious church guys. He was done with those Bible scholars, the well-educated Pharisees, who claimed to know it all and, surprise, did not know God—at all. Jesus hates religion—more than anything else.

Doesn't Jesus hate sin more than religion? Yes, Jesus hates sin, but He took care of sin. Actually, Jesus took all sin away, at a huge price to Himself. He "takes away the sin of the world" (John 1:29 NLT), "as far from us as the east is from the west"

(Psalm 103:12 NLT). When we believe this (and I agree that this can be a challenge to believe), not only will we be free from the grip and power of sin, but we will also be free from religion. Sinners are not the ones Jesus was mad at. He was furious with those pseudo saints and wasted no time telling them they were full of dead men's bones.

Why does Jesus hate religion so much? Religion is repulsive to Jesus. Religion shrinks the cross to a feeble transaction. Religion robs us of real faith. Religion ruins us with fear. Religion rots our insides. Religion reeks of a righteousness that is like filthy rags.

In order to begin to shed this ruse of religion, we need to unmask some lies. Religion is built on lies—powerful lies that contain some truth. That is why they have so much power. Truth, however, is first and foremost a Person. Jesus, "the truth" (John 14:6), wants to live inside us and set us free from the inside out. Jesus moves His own righteousness, His nature and His Spirit into our very being. This is not just "positional" truth but powerful, personal truth that sets us free. Jesus is all about our freedom. Religion is all about bondage. Jesus wants to expose the lies of religion. These false narratives focus on our self-effort and the need to be right. Both produce performance, pretending, pride and the ensuing captivity of exhaustion and fear.

Fear is at the root of religion, including the Christian religion. Fear is religion's primary tool for ensuring obedience and misery. I experienced a mound of misery through the years, perpetrated by a range of religious fears. Fear of disappointing godly parents. Fear of angering a moody God. Fear of being deceived. Fear of failing. Fear of giving the wily devil a place in my life. Fear of missing God's perfect will. Fear of facing a stern Judge and fiery flames forever. Fear of not having enough—enough faith, love or perseverance. Fear of not doing enough—enough praying, fasting, serving. Fear of not being enough—obedient, submissive, spiritual.

Enough of all that fear. Fear enslaves. Fear empowers religion to be a cruel taskmaster. I have felt this religious whip, which inflicts the painful welts of worthlessness. Jesus longs for each of us to lose our religion and to find Him. He wants us to be free of fear and be the actual home of Him who tells us again and again, "Do not fear." Jesus is the One whose unfailing love casts out all fear (see 1 John 4:19). When you experience Him in that way, you will see yourself reflected in Him—free of religion, free of fear and full of His goodness. Losing my religion and helping you lose yours is one of my life's passions. I think Jesus would agree as evidenced by His own Passion, His suffering, to set us free from the bondage and brutality of religion.

Where have you battled fear? Where did it first take root in your soul? How has religion fostered that fear? Listen to the lyrics sung by Lauren Daigle in her song "Losing My Religion."[2] Grab your phone and download this powerful song. The words are an anthem to the journey of finally losing one's religion and getting set free from the fear that forges facades—facades that destroy our true faith in Jesus.

Fear forced me into a masquerade. A Christian charade. A play of pretending that I thought pleased God and convinced Him of my goodness. I performed in this religious drama for too long. I no longer feel forced to play a role, although I am pretty good at acting. Being a good actress is not helpful when you want to be the most authentic you. But "fake" is more important than "faith" when it comes to religion. Just "fake it till you make it" chimes the cheery, yet chilling, voice of fear. Playing a role is exhausting. Playing a role is wrong. Playing a role riles anger, a righteous anger against putrid performance.

We all have some of religion's tentacles wrapped around us. Our enemy's name is the devil, the liar, and his tentacles smother the life of Christ in us. These tentacles are lies—religious tenets that promise security and salvation if we obey. They pressure us to perform for a God who is hard to please. They terrorize us with the fear that our performance does not pass His score-keeping scrutiny. Or they swell our heads with pride over the fact that our performance is far superior to those around us. But we no longer have to perform. We no longer have to be a terrified victim on the religious stage of life. Nor do we need to prance and primp for the applause of people or God. The final curtain has fallen. Yes, the curtain in the temple "was torn in two, from top to bottom" (Mark 15:38) because perfect performance was impossible. Jesus was the perfect and final sacrifice. "Just as the veil was torn in two, Jesus' body was torn open to give us free and fresh access to him" forever (Hebrews 10:20 TPT); therefore, we can draw closer to God "with an open heart, fully convinced by faith that nothing will keep us at a distance from him" (verse 22 TPT).

We live freely, loved in His presence, clean inside and out. Ask Him to dismantle the lies that stunt your growth. Listen for His words that bring true transformation. Be changed from the inside out. Be free of religion at last. Be who He has made you to be in union with Him.

A DIY People in an HGTV World

"Lose your life! Pick up your cross! Die daily!"

Lies.

What? These are words spoken by Jesus.

Yes, and these are words misspoken by religious zealots through the years, twisting what Jesus meant. Religion demands that we sacrifice—sacrifice ourselves and our lives. We must pick up our cross and die, daily, by the way. These words have pounded in my aching head and ripped against my weary heart. Sometimes they were shouted by angry preachers. Sometimes they echoed off the pages of dead authors. These words haunted me. I wanted to be a good disciple of Jesus. I tried hard to lose my life. I did my share of dying via the disciplines. Yet, I failed to truly die.

Do I believe disciples should forsake the disciplines?

No. Jesus was a man of discipline and modeled this for His followers. Likewise, I have learned from many disciplined people and their honest accounts of trying to get on the altar, carry their cross, crucify the flesh, and practice fasting, praying and reading the Bible. I have also learned that dying to self can make me more miserable, callous and ultimately, the most cynical religious robot. I never want to join these ranks. I almost did. I was snared by religion. I was caught in the trap of crucifying my own self via my own self-efforts. How ironic! I have observed this same snare in others because we are DIY (do-it-yourself) people.

We are eager to do it ourselves, whether that is a full bathroom-tile redo or a one-hour paint job of that naked Ikea bookshelf. Think about all those HGTV shows that display such amazing renovation results—all accomplished in sixty minutes or less. Somehow, that DIY mindset creeps into our relationship with God. In my attempts to "do it myself," I missed the irony of all my attempts to get rid of self. I was trying so hard to lose the very self that was producing all the self-effort to lose myself. (Did I just lose you with all that self-talk?) In my attempts to lose myself, I almost lost my mind. Worse, I almost lost my faith. I was burned out on religion. I did not need to lose my life, and I certainly did not need to lose my mind or my faith.

I needed to lose my religion instead. Thank God, I lost my religion and found Jesus. Jesus is good at showing us how to lose our religion. He did not come to start a new religion. He came to give us life. Abundant life. And religion offers us the opposite. We wear out. We give up. We join the "nones"—no faith at all. This is Jesus' invitation to us:

> "Are you tired? Worn out? Burned out on religion? Come to me. Get away with me and you'll recover your life. I'll show you how to take a real rest. Walk with me and work with me—watch how I do it. Learn the unforced rhythms of grace. I won't lay anything heavy or ill-fitting on you. Keep company with me and you'll learn to live freely and lightly."
>
> Matthew 11:28–30 MSG

Soak in that Scripture. Let the words wash over your weary soul. Take a bath, and find real rest, with Jesus. Add some bubbles and candles, too, so you can relax and stop all that weary work of religion. Jesus knows religion destroys us. He invites us to come and learn from Him how to embrace our union with Him. This is a union that provides rest, freedom, delight and lots of love and grace. Jesus loves to walk and work with us in a way that is exhilarating, not exhausting. Anytime we begin to feel worn out, it is a warning that religion has wormed its way back into our rhythm of life. Simply stop and rest, rest from religion's demand to do more, try harder and give up all. Jesus does require us to give up something. He requires us to give up one of religion's primary tools—our self-effort. This is not the same as giving up our very self. The difference is critical.

In my desire to be a true disciple of Jesus, I studied and preached on His most important discipleship teachings. Luke wrote one of Jesus' most famous passages about the cost of discipleship:

> Now great crowds accompanied him, and he turned and said to them, "If anyone comes to me and does not hate his own father and mother and wife and children and brothers and sisters, yes, and even his own life, he cannot be my disciple. Whoever does not bear his own cross and come after me cannot be my disciple. For which of you, desiring to build a tower, does not first sit down and count the cost, whether he has enough to complete it? Otherwise, when he has laid a foundation and is not able to finish, all who see it begin to mock him, saying, 'This man began to build and was not able to finish.' Or what king, going out to encounter another king in war, will not sit down first and deliberate whether he is able with ten thousand to meet him who comes against him with twenty thousand? And if not, while the other is yet a great way off, he sends a delegation and asks for terms of peace. So therefore, any one of you who does not renounce all that he has cannot be my disciple."
>
> Luke 14:25–33

As I stood before the congregation, I issued this sober challenge in my most intense "you better behave" voice: "Who among us is willing to count the cost, the severe and sacrificial cost to follow Jesus? Who is willing to pay the price?" I proceeded to preach on the Luke passage with plenty of admonitions to get serious, really serious, if you were a true disciple of Jesus. Serious enough to sacrifice everything. Serious enough to renounce it all. I was *serious*.

Shame flooded the room. People shifted in their seats as the weight of the message hit their hearts. I let the impact of the sermon sink in as I swelled a bit with pride at my success in delivering a powerful word. Except, it was not a true word. I know it appears that way at first glance. But that first glance is from reading the text with religious eyes of self-effort. I directed people to look at self and see if each "self" had enough effort to do what Jesus asked. That challenge is okay, but that is only half the message.

What is the full, true message? Count the cost? Yes, please do count the cost of finishing what you are building and you will see you do not have nearly enough to finish. Yes, count the cost of going to battle against the enemy and see that you do not have enough to win even a tiny battle, let alone the entire war.

Do you see that self is completely inadequate? Do you see that self-effort will not get the job done? But this should not depress you. Your inadequacy should not cause you to despair. This is not a time to suck it up and try harder. On the contrary, such revelations about our lack and our inability show us something amazing. We need a Savior. He pays the cost, not us. We do not have what it takes. We do not have enough effort, but He does. Without Him, we can build nothing. Without Him, we can never win a battle and certainly not a war. Now, with that inventory and assessment, it is pretty easy to renounce all—all our measly, pathetic self-efforts that can do nothing. We can pick up that cross where all that self-effort just died and follow Him. We can lose the lie that we had to have enough. Jesus has everything we need to build for completion and to beat the enemy in every battle.

Look to Him, not to yourself. We live in union with Him. We are true disciples of Jesus. He teaches us to live freely, lightly, trusting in Him and not in ourselves and our resources. Jesus is bigger, better and more beautiful than we ever knew. But that does not mean that we are smaller, "worse-er" and uglier than we already thought. Such self-loathing is just another prevalent and harmful manifestation of the religious self-effort in our lives. Instead of rearing its ugly head, this time our self-effort works hard to hang its head low, as low as it can go, smack-dab into a giant pool of self-pity.

Embracing Your True Identity

"O Lord! I am so unworthy. Such a lowly worm. Have mercy on me!"

I have said these words. I have sung these words. God forgive me.

What? Isn't it good to pour out our hearts to God in this way? Isn't it good to be honest?

Maybe—if we do not know Him and the price He paid for us.

Maybe—if we want to deny the truth of Scripture and continue to live under the old covenant.

Maybe—if we want to be miserable.

But our Father sees us as valuable, worthy, deeply loved and accepted. There is no room for self-pity. Self-pity is deceptive and debilitating. Self-pity pretends to be humility. Self-loathing sounds so pious and meek and . . . pitiful. Self-pity is a sin. This is a relatively easy religious ritual to get rid of. Jesus told me, *Just stop it*. Yep, that's it. *Just stop it.*

Stop illegitimate lamenting (there are some legit reasons). Stop feeling sorry for yourself. Stop throwing a party, a pity party, that no one else wants to attend, including God. Stop whining and begging God to do something He has already done—forgiven all your sins and lavished mercy on you. Stop singing songs that do not celebrate our resurrected Savior. Just stop sinning and start thanking Jesus.

So I did what Jesus said to do; I discovered the liberating truth that I am enough. I lost the lie that I will never measure up. I stopped believing a big religious lie that says He has not already done enough. That we somehow have to do our part to complete His sacrifice. The truth is, it is finished. Jesus finished the work. Our work, no matter how good or how bad, cannot change that.

Start celebrating who He is, all He has done and who He has made you to be. Don't feel like it? That is why we live by faith (that is not the same as fake). We can choose to believe with our hearts and confess with our mouths that Jesus is Lord and King in our lives now, no matter the circumstances or situation. We can rest and rejoice in Him.

But I must truly believe Jesus is Lord, not me. I know we say this, but our current culture seduces us with a search for significance, a search for the real me. And religion is right there, ready to offer an attractive alternative to our union with Christ. The search for the "real me" is rampant in our culture and in our churches. The question of the century is *Who am I?* And the Christian religion has hopped on the identity bandwagon.

Contemporary Christianity sanitizes death of self with this fresh emphasis on identity—a popular topic in Christian publishing, music and teaching with many resources available. The religion of identity has thousands of worshipers. Many struggle to "find me." Pursuit of identity (as in *my* identity, *my* destiny, *my* gifting, calling, ministry, etc.) becomes an idol with a capital *I*. Many strive on Instagram, Twitter and Facebook to establish a successful self, a cool identity—a God lover to be sure but a self-promoter who begs you to like her latest post. Then many stumble. Some stumble harder than others. Increasing numbers of young and old have taken their own lives. Death to self takes a twisted turn. Religion is ruthless. The religion of DIY. The religion of success. The religion of identity.

Asking *Who am I?* is fine. But the answer to that question must begin with, "I am one who lives in union with I AM." That sounds a bit confusing, but it is critical. The search for the real you must commence with the truth that Christ lives in you. Otherwise, we start a discovery process or extreme makeover job that leaves Jesus on the side and self in charge once again. We must lose the lie that says, *I have to find myself, and I have to discover the real me.* If we do not lose this lie, we will spend years discerning and then discarding the false self with all our self-efforts. Religion grips us again and we succumb to death by burnout.

Meanwhile, Jesus waits for us to discover the secret to the Christian life—I AM living in me. We are privileged, right now, to enjoy a union with the One who says: *I am the Bread of Life, living water, Light of the world and the good Shepherd.* The Great I AM lives in me. Christ in me and me in Christ. While it takes a lifetime (probably an eternity) to plunge the depths of this union and the discovery of our identity as one with Jesus, we retain our unique personalities as we learn to know Him more. There are no Christian clones, contrary to religion's attempts to produce proselytes. God gave each of us a beautiful one-of-a-kind personality, and our real identity can only be lived out in union with Him, the Great I AM.

Jesus shows you how to embrace your true identity as a righteous, "holy and blameless" (Ephesians 1:4), much-loved and accepted son or daughter of God (see Romans 8:29–30). This is your God-given identity. This is not your Facebook-enhanced bio. This is the real righteous you, the real righteous me. This is the truth that will set us free—free from religion's stranglehold that demands we get it right. We are righteous. Woo-hoo! Religion has done a big number on this one. At most, religion will let you put on a coat of righteousness to cover up your dirty, sinful self. Jesus is our righteousness, and He lives in us.

All of us, made in God's image, have an innate desire to be right. We want to be right in our beliefs, our behavior and our lives—right in our very being. We are obsessed with being right. And that is not wrong. God created us that way. We want to be right, and that is right. But it can be wrong to be right. I have lots of experience with this one. Stick with me, all right? This is an ancient problem that began all the way back in the Garden of Eden. Adam and Eve were explicitly told, "You must not eat from the tree of the knowledge of good and evil" (Genesis 2:17 NIV). But the temptation to be right, the temptation to be wise and know it all, was powerful back then. And it is today. We want to be right. It feels so right and so in control. It just happens to be so wrong. We learned this difficult lesson with no little difficulty ourselves.

A Relational Faith First, Then Doctrinal

From the time my husband and I planted our church, we had a deep desire to lead our people in the right path. We both had our eyes opened to how wrong we had believed before we were filled with the Holy Spirit. We were eager to finally get it right and teach others to do the same. We were one hundred percent committed to discerning doctrinal truth, but that desire took us on a dangerous detour. This is not to say doctrines are unimportant, because they are important. But our faith is in a Person, not a principle, deity or doctrine. Our faith is a relational faith first, a doctrinal faith second. If we do not get the relationship right, we are doomed to doctrinal death. We want to have the right beliefs, but "even the demons believe" (James 2:19).

We wanted to be right in order to please God. We did not know He was already pleased, already totally satisfied with Jesus' work for us. Our determination to be right was focusing more on our ability and not on Jesus' work. We wasted a lot of energy, and, I am sad to admit, we even wasted some people's lives. It was not long on this road to rightness before we were crossing every *t* and dotting every *i* and making everyone uptight and miserable with our nitpicky rightness. We had to be right on baptism, prayer, communion, tithing, dress, Bible study, parenting, marriage, drinking, doctors, fasting and the list went on and on. We became proud, obnoxious, unhappy pastors—"frauds and pretenders" (Matthew 23:15 TPT). And our people were twice as miserable.

In addition, I suffered from one of the worst side effects of religion and getting it right. I had excruciating pain from pretending—pretending I was joyful because it was only "right" to rejoice always. Pretending I was unafraid because it was "right" to fear not. Pretending I loved that nasty, critical curmudgeon because it was "right" to love your enemies. My face ached from smiling a fake smile. Worse was the weight of fear on my whole being—fear of being wrong, fear of displeasing God and fear of being an open target for the devil's attacks because I was not believing right. It can be wrong to be right.

Thankfully, the Holy Spirit intervened. He showed us it was far more important to our Father, first of all, to be real. More important than being right. That seemed wrong, but I wondered, *Can I be real with God?* God knows my deepest heart and mind, but somehow, I had fallen into thinking I could fake it with God. My fake joy did not fool Him. My fake love did not fool Him. My fake peace did not hide my fear and worry from Him. My fake holiness, generated by woeful willpower, certainly did not deceive or please Him. I could be real. I could share my heart, my fears, my frustrations, my failures. Not another pity party—just a personal, intimate, real conversation with Papa. I could pour out my heart to Him without fear of disapproval. He loved me unconditionally. He did not demand nor expect me to be one hundred percent doctrinally right. I was right in my relationship with Him through my faith in Jesus, not via my right beliefs. I was right and righteous in His eyes with the righteousness of Jesus.

This is pivotal for our freedom and our ability to finally lose our religion and all its lies. This is the foundation we need to finally find Jesus, Truth Himself. I was set free, wrecked for God, by the truth. I could lose the lie that I had to be right. Instead, I could be real with God. He could then show me lovingly what is right and empower me to walk in the right way. I could lose the fear of deception, because the Holy Spirit is the "Spirit of truth" (John 14:17) who leads and guides me into all truth.[3] I could not keep myself from the evil one's lies, but the Holy Spirit could. Once again, my focus had been on my own self, not on my Savior, Jesus.

I was trying to be all He said I was—joyful, loving, peaceful, holy and right. Yet I was trying to do this apart from Him and my union with Him. I was trusting in myself, not trusting in Jesus. I was trusting my work, not His. Sure, my motivation was to obey Him, do as He said, be who He said I was and live a good Christian life. But my method was self-effort. Self-effort is religion at its finest and fiercest. God desired my faith in Him and His love. God did not want my feeble attempts performed in fear. I had to lose my religion to find Jesus. He was already living in me, fully pleased with me as a righteous, deeply loved, accepted daughter of God.

This basic truth of "how to be a Christian without being religious" affects so many aspects of our daily life as a disciple of Jesus.

Religion says you have to work hard to fight your old nature.

Jesus says, *I give you a new heart.*

Religion says to diligently strive to be close to Jesus.

Jesus says, *We are already one.*

Religion says if you obey, you will be blessed.

Jesus says, *If you trust Me, you will be blessed.*

Religion fills us with shame, condemnation and guilt.

Jesus fills us with Himself and freedom.

He wants to live in union with us.

"For you were included in the death of Christ and have died with him to the religious system and powers of this world. Don't retreat back to being bullied by the standards and opinions of religion" (Colossians 2:20 TPT). I have died to religion. No turning back for me. I have been wrecked for God and for good. I will not be bullied or burned out by religion ever again.

You can enjoy this transformation, too. You can say yes to Jesus' invitation in Matthew 11:28: "Are you tired? Worn out? Burned out on religion? Come to me" (MSG).

Why Does This Matter?

Religion ruins us with its ruthless, relentless demand to be a better self. Jesus redeems us with His own body and blood so we can be our true transformed selves. This is our ultimate desire, birthed in us by our Father and made possible by our union with Him. We must choose to be ruthless and relentless in losing our religion and finding the Redeemer, hidden within. "For you died to this life, and your real life is hidden with Christ in God" (Colossians 3:3 NLT). He is ready to reveal our real life, filled with laughter, love and a forever faith.

What Can I Do Right Now?

Don't waste another minute. Remove the noose of religion from your neck before you lose your life of faith. Refuse to be in bondage to religion's captivity of fear. Receive Jesus' freedom by faith in Him and His love for you.

Father, please empower me to rest in Your unfailing love that casts out all fear.

— 3 —

Life, Not Death

Jesus is the Living Word.
Don't let the Bible "kill" you.

THE BIBLE CAN BE HARD TO UNDERSTAND, DIFFICULT
TO APPLY AND EVEN HURTFUL.

He was a well-known Christian preacher with the title "apostle."
I was honored to have him at my dinner table and eager to hear
what he had to say. I was excited to serve my special homemade
rhubarb dessert along with steaming cups of coffee as we settled
in for some deep conversation about the Bible and our faith.

To my surprise he said, "The women can finish up in the
kitchen now. We men will carry on here." I was confused. Did
he mean me? I guess, since I was the only woman in the dining
room. Shaken and embarrassed, I cleared some empty plates
and fled to the kitchen.

*The women can finish up in the kitchen now. We men will
carry on here.*

Those words hurt. A part of me died as those words pierced
my soul. A sliver of my self-worth shriveled. I was filled with

shame and confusion once more. My poor husband was bewildered. I did not blame him. He did not agree with the apostle's attitude at all but tried to honor him as our guest.

Once again, I was the victim of someone's twisted Bible understanding. Someone who was older and "smarter." Someone who claimed to know what the Bible said: *Women should be silent. Women should submit. Women are second-class Christians.* The Bible, wielded like a slashing sword and grossly misinterpreted, can kill.

Don't Let the Bible Kill You

Jesus said, "The words I speak to you are Spirit and life. But there are still some of you who won't believe" (John 6:63 TPT). Since He is the Living Word, His voice needs to be heard over the thousands of other Bible commentators and scholars who love to announce with deep-voiced authority, "The Bible says . . ." The Bible does not talk in a literal sense, but Jesus does. We want to hear the voice of the good Shepherd. His words are Spirit and life.

The Bible is an important part of that hearing, for sure. But the Bible is not easy to read, hear or heed. I hope to compel you to reexamine your approach to the Bible—to read your Bible and fall in love with Jesus all over again. I want your Bible reading to give you life—a life you are eager to live every day with Christ in you. Jesus, the Living Word, brings life. This is an honorable, uplifting life that He has brought to me and to countless others, especially women.

Read the gospels. Listen and watch as Jesus loves women, heals women, forgives women, calls women to follow Him. Then, shock of all shocks, Jesus chooses a woman. At a time in history when women were oppressed and ridiculed and would never be considered reliable witnesses to anything, Jesus chooses a woman, Mary Magdalene, as the first witness to announce the most important news the world has ever heard. Jesus sends Mary to tell the men that He has risen from the dead (see John 20:17–18).

He is alive to bring life to all. When we read the Bible in union with Jesus, we feel so alive. We feel loved and affirmed. He speaks hard things to us, too, so we avoid going down paths that lead to death. He wants us to love reading the Bible, to hear Him speak and to receive life from His words—words of love, acceptance and encouragement. But that is more the exception than the rule. Why? Because the Bible can "kill."

Read your church history book. Scriptures have been used for centuries to justify some of the greatest crimes. Africans have been cruelly enslaved, women have endured extreme physical and emotional abuse, people have been tortured, beheaded, drowned and burned at the stake—all because of the Bible. Well-meaning believers (so they say) used Bible verses to justify such heinous action. I will not dissect church history, although I encourage my readers to get acquainted with an accurate picture of where we have been, especially regarding the Bible.

Those who do not know history are doomed to repeat it. Our history with the Bible has been bloody and—would you agree—deadly? While most of us have not experienced that type of terrible trauma, we have experienced the Bible in negative ways when others have used it against us. Or maybe we have read the Bible and been confused or condemned by its contents. Either way, Jesus wants us to be healed of damage done by teachers and preachers who were flat-out wrong.

Preachers and others have used Scripture as a scalpel to cut me to the core. They have tried to cut off my calling as a female leader just like the apostle in my dining room tried to do, using select Bible texts about women being silent (see 1 Corinthians 14:34). Some have used the Bible to cut out my hope for the healing miracle I desperately needed. Using 1 Corinthians 13:9, they insisted that the gifts described in the Bible had now ceased and God was no longer doing miracles. Others, on a less serious note, have tried to cut off my practice of wearing beautiful linen pants with a text that forbade me to wear "men's clothing" (see Deuteronomy 22:5). Still others demanded I remove my wedding ring, saying that "the putting on of gold jewelry" (1 Peter 3:3) marked me as a gaudy heathen instead of a godly wife.

Think for a moment of your own negative, not-so-life-giving experiences with the Bible. Have they diminished your desire to read the Bible? Jesus wants our experience with the Bible to bring us life, not death. Jesus, the Living Word, knows that "the letter of the law kills, but the Spirit pours out life" (2 Corinthians 3:6 TPT).

Don't let the Bible kill you. Why continue to do something that beats you up, rather than builds you up? Why continue to listen to Bible teachers who leave you feeling more dead than alive? If you have ever left a church service, Christian conference, Bible conversation or even your own quiet time feeling like a spiritual sluggard, then I invite you to keep reading. I have many "word wounds" and have sadly inflicted some on others. Learn from my Bible bruises. This lesson will wreck your life—for good. I want you to love your Bible, enjoy your Bible and, yes, understand your Bible. But despite having more Bible aids than ever, few people are reading the Bible these days. This is tragic, but true.

Surveys show that the Bible remains one of the least-read, least-understood, least-loved bestsellers of all time. "We might be swimming in millions of Bibles, but we are not a Scripture-soaked society," writes Glenn Paauw in his challenging book, *Saving the Bible from Ourselves: Learning to Read and Live the Bible Well*.[1] He details an underside to the life of the Bible—a story of our frustration, boredom and failed expectations when we commit to a daily quiet time with our Bibles. We read our little spiritual morsel and discover it does not nourish us all that much. After repeated drudgery, we give up reading our Bibles.

Is there something that can change that? You can taste the Living Bread Himself and be truly satisfied. You can discover the Bible is much more than a heavy, hard-to-understand instruction manual. You can experience the Bible as a revelation of Emmanuel—God among us, God inside us. But in order to do that, there is something you must do first.

Do This First

Jesus, addressing some super-smart, Scripture-studying teachers, said:

> "You have your heads in your Bibles constantly because you think you'll find eternal life there. But you miss the forest for the trees. These Scriptures are all about me! And here I am, standing right before you, and you aren't willing to receive from me the life you say you want."
>
> John 5:39–40 MSG

We can have our heads in the Bible. We can read the Bible, study the Bible, memorize the Bible, teach the Bible. But—and this is a big *but*—despite our diligence, we can miss Jesus in the Bible. We can miss the life He offers us. We can miss the love He has for us. That is a scary thought. If we are not seeing Jesus as bigger, better and more beautiful when we read the Scriptures, we need to stop and start over. If we are not seeing the Father more clearly (see John 14:9), we need a fresh way to approach the Bible. If we are being wrecked, but not for God, it is time for a change. If we are more dead than alive, we need help.

So I challenge you to "do this first." This is something that changed my life in every way, especially the way I read the Bible.

From the moment I became a Christian, I read the Bible, studied the Bible, filled up notebooks about the Bible and listened to sermons on the Bible, but I missed the forest for the trees. I did not see Jesus. I read about Jesus in the Bible. I read about Jesus healing many and doing miracles. As I read, I cried out to Him. I said I knew if He were here like in days of old, He would surely heal my body of the gut-wrenching infertility I battled for over three years with no hope. I said I longed to touch His robe and have His life flow into my dead womb. But my Bible teachers had told me emphatically that Jesus was not here. He was not healing today. Yes, He did that in the Bible, but not in our world. Their words killed my hope. Their words killed the life I felt when I read the written words in the Bible and saw Jesus, the Living Word.

Then my life turned upside down and inside out. Despite warnings from smart Bible teachers and Christian cult watchers, I did the one thing that to me is the nonnegotiable if you are ever going to love the Bible, understand the Bible and, most importantly, love Jesus more. Although these Bible thumpers told me to beware of fanaticism, I humbled myself and received a powerful baptism in the Holy Spirit. I became a Holy

Spirit–filled believer, and things have never been the same. Immediately, my experience with the Bible changed. I opened the Bible and began to read, and scales fell off my eyes.

What did I see? Did I understand the Greek and Hebrew better? Did I grasp all that deep theology of the apostle Paul? Did I "get" the end time prophecies?

None of the above.

After I received my first baptism in the Holy Spirit, my blind eyes were opened, and I saw Jesus. I saw that He is "the same yesterday, today, and forever" (Hebrews 13:8 NLT). I saw Jesus still heals barren wombs and still does miracles. I saw Jesus is bigger, better and more beautiful than I had ever imagined. I once was blind, and now I could see.

Do this first. Receive the Holy Spirit. Yes, if you are a believer, you have the Holy Spirit, but Jesus taught us to be immersed, baptized into His Spirit—the Teacher. This makes all the difference. His favorite job: reveal more of Jesus to us (see John 14:26). Stop right now and invite the Holy Spirit to baptize you, fill you and be your Teacher. He is happy to do just that. Hold out your hands and welcome Him to soak every cell of your mind and body. When you read your Bible, count on Him to reveal Jesus. And remember to pick those scales up off the floor.

Read the Bible in Fresh Ways

Now that you have the Holy Spirit as your Teacher, you need new and healthy ways of reading the Bible. I would start with a fresh, readable Bible translation. I love the tried and true NASB, ESV and NLT translations. In order to approach the Bible with fresh eyes, however, try a different translation or paraphrase. This helps jar us out of our old ways of reading and understanding the Bible. We stop skimming. We stop thinking, *Oh, I know what that verse says*. I highly recommend grabbing or downloading *The Passion Translation* if you want to see what union with Christ—God's best secret—is all about. Trust me, you will only be a few verses into Ephesians, and renewed passion for Jesus will flood your heart.

Other translations/paraphrases of the Bible that have brought renewal to my Bible reading and a deeper love of Jesus are *The Message* and *The Living Bible*. These are not study Bibles per se, but they are written with the focus on Jesus and are sure to make you more alive than ever. Are these versions controversial? Yes. There are plenty of naysayers who vehemently critique these Bibles. How sad. A simple test when reading these: Did you find yourself more in love with Jesus? Did you want to obey Him more than ever? If your answer is yes, then read on.

Do invite the Holy Spirit, the Spirit of truth, to read with you, sort out the inedible and highlight the Living Bread that will nourish your soul. Jesus was clear that every word He spoke was a Spirit word—full of life, not death (see John 6:63). Jesus is the Living Word. He brings understanding to the written Word. He has taught me some important ways to read and study the Bible so I can know Him more, not just know more of the Bible or even more about Jesus Himself. He has become bigger, better and more beautiful. Meanwhile, the Bible is not bigger, better nor more beautiful to many readers. It continues to kill and confuse.

Why is the Bible so confusing? For starters, the Bible is one book, but it contains 66 books of many different genres—poetry, narrative, wisdom, prophecy and more. While the Bible was inspired by God, it was written by human authors—including a shepherd, a teacher, a warrior, a doctor and a fisherman, to name a few. And that is not all. The Bible is divided into two parts, the Old and New Testaments, but is not in chronological order. Different authors, different genres, out of order, old and new. Who can read such a book? Yes, the Bible can be mind-boggling and mysterious, but I assure you, it is not a myth.

The Bible is one hundred percent true. At the same time, please note the prepositions *for* and *to* in the following state-ment: "The entire Bible is written for you, but not all of it is written to you."[2] This fact alone will clear up much of your Bible reading confusion. Let me state it again: *Not all of the Bible is written to you, but all of the Bible is written for you.* When you understand this fact, much of your confusion dissipates.

For example, the Old Testament was not written to us as believers in Jesus. Do we throw out the Old Testament because it was not written to us? No way. There is much value in the entire story of God. There are many lessons for us in every book of the Bible. Again, all of the Bible is written for us, including the Old Testament, and we can learn valuable truths from the whole Bible.

A favorite part of the Bible for me is the book of Psalms. I love to pray many of these beautiful songs. Yes, they are part of the Old Testament, but that never stopped me. A favorite psalm for me has been Psalm 51. Here David famously (or should I say, infamously) repents for his horrible, guilt-producing sin. Many of us can identify with his lament, but I hope not with his crimes—murder and adultery. Pretty serious sin. Nevertheless, we do love to pray along with him when we, too, have missed the mark: "Create in me a clean heart, O God. Take not your Holy Spirit from me."

You might ask, *What is wrong with that, Di? Isn't it good to repent and cry out to God when we have sinned?*

Yes and no.

Yes, it is good to talk with God to restore our damaged relationship, but not by using words that negate the finished work of Jesus on the cross. Jesus already created in you and me a clean heart. That was the power and price of His shed blood and broken body. To beg Him to do that again, well, that is almost blasphemous, as if to implore Him not to take away His Spirit when He so clearly said that His Spirit will "be with you forever" (John 14:16).

Whoa! Are we calling Jesus a liar?

Now, I know I may sound extreme here, but this made so much of a difference in my life. I stopped reading and praying this psalm as if it were written to me and began to pray it *for* me—as one who already had a clean heart. I was sorry I acted the opposite of who Jesus had made me to be. I thanked Jesus that He would not take His Spirit from me despite my sinful behavior. After all, that was when I really needed the Spirit's help—to empower me to overcome sin. I turned from my sinful behavior and trusted the Spirit to fill me again. When I read and prayed Psalm 51 (and many others) in this way, I was wrecked for God. I loved Jesus even more for all He had done for me and for who He had made me to be as a new, clean creation, in union with Him. Yes, Psalm 51 was written *for* me, but not *to* me.

Let's take a quick look at a few more Bible texts in order to see how important it is that not all of the Bible is written to us. God told Joshua, "Jericho and everything in it must be completely destroyed" (Joshua 6:17 NLT)—every man, woman and child. Wow! That is violent. Is that written to us? Are we sent to wreak havoc on a city? No! That was not written to us, and we probably never thought it was.

Here is another example that may be more confusing. Jesus said to a young entrepreneur: "Sell all your possessions and give the money to the poor. . . . Then come, follow me" (Matthew 19:21 NLT). Do we do the same? Was this written to us or for us? Watch your answer. It makes a difference—a big, expensive difference.

Paul said to the women in Corinth: "Make sure you cover your head when you pray or prophesy. . . . And remember to stay silent" (see 1 Corinthians 11:5; 14:34). If that is written to us, ladies, then please, we need to put that covering on our heads and shut up. Oh, except when we open our mouth to pray or prophesy (see 1 Corinthians 11:5). That is double-talk.

I could list quite a few more—kiss one another hello (everybody?), treat slaves well (not free them?), keep the Sabbath holy and observe Passover (follow Jewish injunctions?).[3] You get the point. The Bible is confusing when we think it is all written to us and try to live it as such. Most of us would be dead—stoned as teens because we talked back to our parents[4] if all the Bible were written to us.

Even though we can easily see the point with these texts, many people continue to be "conned." How? They hear these texts taught, but the texts are taken out of context. If we ignore the context of Scripture, we will certainly be conned. We can think a text is written *to* us when it was written *for* us.

Can we learn from all these Bible texts?

Absolutely. There are lessons for us, but not directly to us.

Put on Son Glasses

In order to get a fuller grasp on this important shift in our approach to the Bible, we need an understanding of the covenants.

Covenants are important in the Bible. They refer to and describe the way God and humans relate to one another. Covenants are the ultimate DTR (define the relationship) tool. I highly recommend Jonathan Welton's book *Understanding the Whole Bible* (Welton Academy, 2015) for its valuable teaching on the different covenants in the Bible (there are more than two).

The most important covenant for our understanding is the New Covenant—made between the Father and Jesus and enacted by Jesus' shed blood and broken body (see Matthew 26:26–29). This same Jesus lives in us. We are in union with Him and included in this amazing covenant. This changes how we read the Bible, what it says to us and the life it gives us, especially the life we have in union with Christ Jesus. This New Covenant, out of all the covenants in the Bible, is the one written to us. The others are written for us, and yes, we can learn from them, but they do not define the relationship we have with God in our union with Jesus.

But as with our physical eyes, we often need new glasses—spiritual glasses—in order to read more clearly, with more focus and with an enhanced ability to see Christ in us, in the Scriptures. I like to recommend Son glasses, which is a metaphor for spiritual glasses, if you will. This is a way to read the Bible through the lens of Jesus, the Son, and His finished work on our behalf. These Son glasses are as valuable as the knowledge that not all the Bible is written to us and the revelation of the New Covenant.

Jesus provided Son glasses for the two folks on the Emmaus road right after His resurrection. You might remember the story of these two who were walking along in deep despair and animated conversation (see Luke 24). They were perplexed about the disturbing events of the recent crucifixion, and now purported resurrection, of the miracle-working prophet Jesus. They were saddened and confused. They thought they knew their Bibles. But things did not look at all like they expected. Then the resurrected Jesus joined their conversation but kept His identity hidden.

He did offer them Son glasses. He gave them the priceless ability to see the Scriptures from a different perspective, the perspective of Himself, the Son of God, when He told them, "Why are you so thick-headed? Why do you find it so hard to believe every word the prophets have spoken? Wasn't it necessary for Christ, the Messiah, to experience all these sufferings and then afterward to enter into his glory?" (verses 25–26 TPT).

Yes, we have been thick-headed. Yes, we have found it hard to believe the full and glorious truth that the cross was a smashing success.

"Then he carefully unveiled to them the revelation of himself throughout the Scripture. He started from the beginning and explained the writings of Moses and all the prophets, showing how they wrote of him and revealed the truth about himself" (verse 27 TPT). We need the Son's revelation of the words we have known, but not seen.

Now we see You, Jesus. We see You in all the Bible. We believe.

And just like those two friends, we say: "Why didn't we recognize it was him? Didn't our hearts burn with the flames of holy passion while we walked beside him? He unveiled for us such profound revelation from the Scriptures!" (verse 32 TPT).

That is what happens when we wear Son glasses—when we read the Scriptures in union with Jesus, when He unveils profound revelation from God's Word. When He shows us texts we have known, memorized and thought we understood, but we needed His Son glasses to clarify the truth. Here is one illustration of this from my own life.

I loved Jesus' parables of the hidden treasure and the precious pearl. I loved to preach on this text and exhort us to give up everything, to sell all we possessed to get Jesus, the precious pearl, the hidden treasure, and to do this with overflowing joy. "Nothing," I proclaimed, "nothing should stand in the way of our possessing Jesus, the pearl of great price."

Emotions were stirred. Tears were shed. And of course, plenty of guilt flooded those who knew they were not desperate enough to give up all. I am here to humbly say, I was wrong. I think that parable can be taught with the above interpretation, but I now believe I did not see a deeper truth. I needed my Son glasses.

Jesus used stories to "illustrate spiritual truths" (Matthew 13:3 TPT). Sitting by the lakeside, for example, He taught about the Kingdom of God: "A person discovered that there was hidden treasure in a field. Upon finding it, he hid it again. Because of uncovering such treasure, he was overjoyed and sold all that he possessed to buy the entire field just so he could have the treasure" (verse 44 TPT). He continued, "Heaven's kingdom realm is also like a jewel merchant in search of rare pearls. When he discovered one very precious and exquisite pearl, he immediately gave up all he had in exchange for it" (verses 45–46 TPT).

You see (and I hope you do), I was making this parable all about me—my effort, my sacrifice, my desperation, my work to obtain the pearl of great price, the hidden treasure of Jesus. When I put on my Son glasses, I saw Jesus. Ah yes, Jesus was the God-man who came to this field called earth. Jesus came seeking us. Jesus "discovered" us, human beings made in His image, and He was overjoyed at this immense treasure of "buried" sons and daughters, dirtied by sin but precious in His sight.

He decided we were so precious, so valuable, that He would give up all, even His own life in exchange for us. He did all the giving up, all the hard work. He made the supreme sacrifice so we could have a restored relationship with Him. We are precious pearls to Jesus. That wrecked me again, for God and for good.

That, my friend, is what the Kingdom of God, not the kingdom of me, is all about. This is how Son glasses change how we see Jesus and how we read His Word. As Jesus got bigger, better and more beautiful in light of all He did for me, I suddenly found myself as bigger, better and more beautiful than I had ever imagined. I saw myself as the treasure, the precious pearl that He saw me as.

Tears? Yes.

Deep emotions? Yes.

Guilt? No. Instead, my heart flowed with fresh, deep love for Jesus. I wanted to give this beautiful Savior my all in all. I wanted to "sell everything I possessed" for Him. I committed again to living in vital union with Him. He is God's best secret.

"And as Christ himself is seen for who he really is, who you really are will also be revealed, for you are now one with him in his glory!" (Colossians 3:4 TPT). There is much more that could be said in this chapter. But this is enough to help you refocus when you read the Bible and see Christ Himself for who He really is. This is enough for you, who are one with Him, to see who you really are. True transformation is sure to come.

Why Does This Matter?

The Bible is a complex, supernatural book—the Father's gift to bring life to us, His children. No wonder the enemy, Satan, seeks to destroy our experiences with the Bible. Now more than ever, we need the Holy Spirit's help for each of us to read, understand and live in the truth of our union with Jesus Christ as revealed in the Bible.

What Can I Do Right Now?

Be filled with the Holy Spirit and invite Him to be your Teacher every time you read the Bible. Remember, not all the Bible is written to you, but all of the Bible is written *for* you. We are part of the New Covenant in union with Jesus. Put on your Son glasses. Get a fresh translation like *The Passion Translation* or *The Message*. Anticipate the revelation of Christ within you. Jesus, the Living Word, will come alive to you.

Father, thank You for the glorious gift of Your Word and the ability to comprehend the truth.

4

Saint Now,
Sinner No More

*Jesus brought you out of the grave.
Embrace the new you, don't fix the old.*

IF I AM NEW AND NO LONGER A SINNER, WHY DO I STILL SIN AND STRUGGLE WITH THE OLD?

As we stared at the open casket of a mutual friend, the person next to me turned to me and asked, "Doesn't he look great?"

Not at all, I thought. (And why do people always say this at funerals?)

"Yes, just like himself," I lied, not wanting to be impolite by disagreeing with a stranger in front of an open casket.

In my opinion, very few dead people look good in a casket. Their eyes are shut (of course, they are dead), but glasses are perched on their nose. The mouth is pursed too tight amid wrinkled skin and lacquered hair. Hands are folded in a most unnatural position. Worst of all is the makeup. Cheeks are too orange, eyebrows are too dark and lips are too red. Makeup on a corpse is morbid. Then why do I continue to put makeup on my corpse?

What? I am not dead. Oh, yes, I am and you are, too, but often we neither realize this nor behave as though it is true. We spend hours trying to fix the old me—the old me that Jesus said is dead. We dissect our past sin, we revisit all the pain and trauma of the old me. We even try to drag that old man around, insisting he behave, willing the old self to be good. But boy, does it stink. That is what corpses do, after all. Much of the Christian focus is on fixing the past that Jesus tells us to forget now that we are made new. I tried to fix the old Dianne. I tried valiantly to put makeup on my corpse, unaware the old me was dead. I thought I was in charge of making sure I was sufficiently crucified, and I wanted to look good in the process.

Then I discovered the old Dianne was dead and I needed to stop putting makeup on my corpse. Jesus did not come, suffer, give His life, shed His blood so I can now have some new tools to fix my past and new principles to help me behave in the present. Jesus did all of the above in order to kill me. Crucify the sinful me. Not a cursory cleanup job. A complete crucifixion. And, thankfully, a real resurrection. And a new Resident within.

Back to funerals . . . I stood before a packed room of mourners at the local funeral home and said, "Although our hearts are filled with sorrow today because we will miss our loved one, Amy, we can take comfort in the fact that Jesus has prepared the perfect room for her in the Father's house." I read Jesus' words in John 14:1–3:

> "Let not your hearts be troubled. Believe in God; believe also in me. In my Father's house are many rooms. If it were not so, would I have told you that I go to prepare a place for you? And

if I go and prepare a place for you, I will come again and will take you to myself, that where I am you may be also."

This is one of the most popular texts preached at funerals, but we have it all wrong. Jesus, on the eve of His death, is not telling His disciples He is leaving to go pick up a hammer and nails so He can build a room for each of us in the Father's heavenly mansion. Instead, Jesus was leaving to die a cruel death and make it possible for us to be where He is—in union with the Father—now.

Won't we have a glorious home in heaven? you may ask.

Yes, someday. But Jesus was proclaiming the shocking truth that His impending death and resurrection would make possible a permanent home for us now, in union with God. Human beings are now the home of God. God has moved right on inside of us.

Are you saying that we become God? Are we now a deity?

This is a legitimate response to the astounding truth of our union with God, who now lives in us. We do not become God. But there is a real ontological (the nature of our being) transformation at our new birth. I am thankful for Greek scholars and academic professionals who have studied this. There are some thorough, but tough to read, texts on the whole topic of union with Christ. Your faith will skyrocket as you read. According to Professor Constantine Campbell, in Greek Orthodox theology,

"divinization" or "deification" means "a literal 'ontological' participation in the being of God," while avoiding any hint of absorption into the divinity with a consequent loss of individual personality. In spite of the strong language of "ontological participation in the being of God," deification does not suggest that believers become God, but that "humans as creatures are introduced into personal relationships of participation in the uncreated, divine energies or grace."[1]

We participate with the divine nature of God without becoming God or losing our personhood. When you read the pages—and years—of study on this challenging topic of union, it gives you confidence to continue your pursuit of such a powerful secret that was hidden for centuries but is now made known. It may be difficult and you may need a dictionary, but it is worth the effort. Whether you read an early Church father like Athanasius or a star theologian like John Calvin, you will find plenty of biblical scholarship to support this surprising secret to true transformation. Hop on Hoopla or Audible and experience that faith comes by hearing. It takes time for faith to strengthen and for this truth to set us free. We have many old mindsets that must go.

Sin Nature Surgery

"Hey, Mom, got a minute?" asked my nineteen-year-old son Cory. His voice was filled with an eagerness that brought immediate relief. He was a big-time football player at a state university and anytime the caller ID flashed his number, fear gripped my stomach.

"Sure!" I said, relaxed and ready for a calm conversation, which turned out to be anything but calm; it was catastrophic. I would not know how catastrophic until later, but his words got my attention.

"Mom, I've been doing some Bible study, and I am really jazzed by what I've learned," he shared.

My heart swelled with pride. My college son loved the Bible. Then he spoke the words that would jolt me out of my comfort and catapult me into a few years of chaos.

"Did you know that we don't have a sin nature?"

What? My son, who seconds before I was worried had a head injury, now spouted the words of a heretic. No longer a sin nature? Cory was a strong Christian, but surely he did not believe, let alone experience, this heresy of "no sin nature." He was a normal teenage male with all the usual college temptations. Was this just an excuse to get away with sinful behavior? What kind of cult had Cory joined now? But it was no cult. Just pure Christianity. Christianity as God intended and the cross made possible.

I was about to discover the astounding truth found all over the New Testament. The "catastrophic" truth or, as some have said, the "scandalous" truth that we are no longer sinners—we are saints. Saints now, sinners no more. How was this possible? I knew I had just sinned that morning, thanks to that crazy driver who had cut me off in traffic. I should really try to sin less. *No*, said the still small voice in my heart. *Not sin less. "Go and sin no more."* I recognized those exact words quoted from John 8:11 (NLT). This was Jesus. He was not just speaking to the woman caught in adultery. He was telling me, *Go and sin no more*. Impossible?

Jesus was about to get bigger, better and more beautiful than I ever imagined. This Jesus who lives in me and gives me a new identity as a saint, not a sinner. This Jesus who tells me to do something that He alone makes possible. He is not in a hurry for us to trust and obey Him here. He knows there is no other way and He is the Way. I am still learning. I know that I am no longer a sinner saved by grace. I am now a saint, empowered by His grace to live as a saint in union with my Savior. This "heresy" wrecked me for good and for God. I am forever grateful to the Son (and son) who set me free.

Why, when we hear such startling statements like, "You no longer have a sin nature" or, "Go and sin no more," do we quickly evaluate whether these are true by our own experience? I mean, I just lied to my desperate friend about my inability to meet. I gossiped with my daughter under the guise of "please pray for Anne's terrible situation," and I snapped at the incompetent sales clerk at Home Depot. Sin nature gone? Nope. My experience screams otherwise. I default to that as my gauge of truth. Experience is an important measurement. We want genuine faith, not one that ignores real life. As I invited the Holy Spirit to lead me into all truth, I was surprised to discover that the Bible reveals that our sin nature was cut off by Jesus.

"When you came to Christ, you were 'circumcised,' but not by a physical procedure. Christ performed a spiritual circumcision—the cutting away of your sinful nature" (Colossians 2:11 NLT). Our sin nature has been circumcised. Circumcised. I have four sons, and believe me, I know what circumcision is. Something is cut off. It is removed. It is not half on and half off. Christ performed a spiritual circumcision, the cutting away of our sinful nature. We no longer have a sin nature. We are not half holy. We are not semi sinner. We are saints, not sinners. So, why do we still sin?

I cannot answer why you do, but I know that it does not take a sin nature to sin. That is right. Adam and Eve did not have a sin nature in the Garden, and yet, they sinned. Big-time! And Jesus was tempted on the mount by Satan and could have made a choice to sin (otherwise it was not really a temptation). Jesus overcame that temptation and began to reveal how sons and daughters are to live here on earth, overcoming sin and Satan, in union with God. It does not take a sin nature to sin. A sin nature makes it easier to sin. But as a believer in Jesus, you no longer have a sin nature. It has been cut off—removed through a tremendous sacrifice of Jesus. That is why it is so tragic that thousands of believers still choose to sin.

> You were dead because of your sins and because your sinful nature was not yet cut away. Then God made you alive with Christ, for he forgave all our sins. He canceled the record of the charges against us and took it away by nailing it to the cross.
>
> Colossians 2:13–14 NLT

Most Christians would agree that Jesus forgives our sin, but I, like so many, did not know that Jesus has already forgiven all my sin—past, present and future. All sins are gone. My sin nature is gone, too. And this is a big deal. Why? Because when we think Jesus just forgives sin and every time we do sin we must confess, get forgiven again and then all is well, the focus is on me and not on Jesus. The focus is on what I do—my work—not on the astounding work of Jesus on the cross when the Lamb of God took away all sin (see John 1:29). He did not just cover up sin or take away only some sin until a future date contingent on our confession of present sin. Our sin nature was cut off. Removed. Gone. We have been born anew. We have a new nature, a new heart and a new Spirit who empowers us to live in our new identity as a saint.

Righteousness Revealed

Jesus did the almost unthinkable: "For our sake he made him to be sin who knew no sin, so that in him we might become the righteousness of God" (2 Corinthians 5:21).

Jesus is our righteousness, and He paid a huge price for us to be equally yoked with Him. And this is no mere "imputation" of righteousness, a Christlike coverup of our still-cruddy self. We take on Christ's righteousness. Michael J. Gorman, an accomplished academic and biblical scholar, writes:

> Although this text is often interpreted as a witness to Paul's (alleged) theology of imputation (the notion that Christ's righteousness is reckoned to sinners), many recent scholars have rightly recognized that this is a text of transformation, and particularly of taking on one of the most fundamental divine attributes: justice/righteousness.[2]

We are made righteous in our being. We are not just given some fake righteousness. We are made righteous. We are a pure, spotless, righteous Bride ready to be joined in union with Jesus. This is more than a mere imputation. This is transformation.

> Our faith in Jesus transfers God's righteousness to us and he now declares us flawless in his eyes. This means we can now enjoy true and lasting peace with God, all because of what our Lord Jesus, the Anointed One, has done for us. Our faith guarantees us permanent access into this marvelous kindness that has given us a perfect relationship with God. What incredible joy bursts forth within us as we keep on celebrating our hope of experiencing God's glory!
>
> Romans 5:1–2 TPT

We believe and learn to live in this tremendous truth, jumping for joy with our righteous new heart.

And yet, for too many years in my life as a Christian, I had the mistaken belief that my new heart was somehow still wicked.

I had been taught (and sadly, even taught this myself) that the heart is sick and I had to work hard to bring health to my new heart.

"The heart is deceitful above all things, and desperately sick; who can understand it?" (Jeremiah 17:9).

That is our old heart. This is why Jesus had to die for us. We have a new heart now—thanks to Jesus. But I thought even my new heart was still sick and wicked. This belief resulted in practices that I thought would make my "wicked" heart better. I prayed, read the Bible, fasted, served others and undertook other practices to help "doctor" my sick heart. I received inner healing prayer to uproot all the wickedness inside me. I am not saying these practices are wrong. But I engaged in them to fix myself. I relied on my work and not on Jesus' work. Jesus made it possible for me to have a totally new heart. Jesus paid an enormous price to make me "a new creation" (2 Corinthians 5:17).

The old wicked heart is gone. We have received new, pure, healthy hearts. Our old sin nature is gone, cut off. We are born anew. We can gain some valuable insight by comparing this to a physical heart transplant. There are many parallels to our receiving new hearts from Jesus. When we receive our new hearts, it is only possible because Someone has died. Someone dies so another can live. Jesus is that Someone. We, like transplant recipients, can do nothing to deserve a new heart. Our old hearts were diseased, and we were dead in sin. We trusted Jesus and received new hearts; the old heart is totally gone. Just like a transplant patient, none of our old diseased heart can remain or that would be fatal. We overflow with thankfulness to our Donor, Jesus. We have a heartfelt determination to live differently—for Him.

But here is the challenge. A person who has major surgery to receive a new heart does not jump up and run a marathon. She learns a whole new way of life with this new heart. She learns to eat and drink differently, exercise regularly, take her meds and rest. She still has the same mind and the same body. She may be tempted to live unwisely or go back to old ways, but that is dangerous. We, too, learn how to live with our new hearts from Jesus. This takes time. Since our minds and bodies are not new, we have to learn new ways of living with new hearts from Jesus. We are not left to ourselves. We each have our own personal trainer—the Holy Spirit. God promises, "I will give you a new heart, and a new spirit I will put within you. And I will remove the heart of stone from your flesh and give you a heart of flesh. And I will put my Spirit within you, and cause you to walk in my statutes and be careful to obey my rules" (Ezekiel 36:26–27).

I will put My Spirit in you. How brilliant! We have our own personal trainer—One who lives in us, empowers us, teaches us and strengthens us to live differently. We choose to interact with and depend on Him. This is not about willpower. This is about Spirit power. We make time to "work out" with Him and receive fresh grace every day. We engage in the practices that will retrain our minds and bodies in regard to our new hearts.

Comprehending the Cross

"Were you there when they crucified my Lord? Oh, it causes me to tremble, tremble, tremble. Were you there when they crucified my Lord?"[3]

The haunting refrain of this beautiful spiritual floated through my mind and stirred my heart as I listened to the gospel choir on

YouTube. These words were originally sung by generations of enslaved African Americans and now flooded me with childhood memories of bygone Easter services where I first struggled with the difficult message of the cross. Why did Jesus die? Why the horrific death of crucifixion? When older, I still struggled although I knew the theological answers. I strained to embrace the utter devastation of the cross. I studied those detailed descriptions of what happens to a body when crucified and the horrible violence of such a death. I watched *The Passion of the Christ* movie multiple times to provoke my thankfulness for all Jesus did. The cross remained an enigma to me. I knew the crucifixion was real. But try as I might, I could not comprehend the cross.

Have you ever strived to be really thankful for Jesus' shed blood and terrible death? I was thankful for the promise of sins forgiven and life eternal with Jesus. When I learned the cross included Jesus taking my sicknesses, I wept with gratitude. When I discovered that Satan was defeated at the cross and the cross was not just a transaction to get me a ticket to heaven, I danced with delight. But I had a nagging sense that something greater occurred at the crucifixion and resurrection. That is where I was that morning, listening to "Were You There," when Jesus spoke these words to me: *You were there, Dianne. You were there when they crucified Me, your Lord.*

What? How could I be there on Calvary? That happened two thousand years ago. Is this some sort of time travel mystery?

No, you were actually there. But you weren't just watching. You were participating. You were crucified with Me, buried with Me, raised with Me. You were there—in Me.

This is when I began to comprehend the most important truth in this whole book (and I dare say, in the whole Bible).

91

We, the sons and daughters made in the image of our Father, yet terribly marred by sin and in desperate need of being made new, were in Christ—in union with Him on that cross, in that grave and on that resurrection morning. We ran out of that grave in Jesus, not with just our sins forgiven, but with our entire being made new. Saint now, sinner no more. It sounds stranger than fiction, but it is a fact. Let that sink in, because it will change your life—if you believe it.

The fuzziness of the cross began to come into focus. My union with Jesus included a real crucifixion and a real resurrection—not only of Jesus, but also of me. This was not just a cleanup of my life, it was a crucifixion of the sinful me. This was not just a repair of my old life, it was a resurrection into a new life. Saint now, sinner no more.

Or have you forgotten that all of us who were immersed into union with Jesus, the Anointed One, were immersed into union with his death?

Sharing in his death by our baptism means that we were co-buried and entombed with him, so that when the Father's glory raised Christ from the dead, we were also raised with him. We have been co-resurrected with him so that we could be empowered to walk in the freshness of new life. For since we are permanently grafted into him to experience a death like his, then we are permanently grafted into him to experience a resurrection like his and the new life that it imparts.

Could it be any clearer that our former identity is now and forever deprived of its power? For we were co-crucified with him to dismantle the stronghold of sin within us, so that we would not continue to live one moment longer submitted to sin's power.

Romans 6:3–6 TPT

Co-crucified? No longer submitted to sin's power? C\
resurrected? Empowered to walk in the freshness of new life?\
Do I understand how all this really happened?

> My old identity has been co-crucified with Messiah and no
> longer lives; for the nails of his cross crucified me with him.
> And now the essence of this new life is no longer mine, for the
> Anointed One lives his life through me—we live in union as one!
> My new life is empowered by the faith of the Son of God who
> loves me so much that he gave himself for me, and dispenses
> his life into mine!
>
> Galatians 2:20 TPT

The nails of His cross crucified me with Him. He lives His life
through me. We live in union as one. Almost incomprehensible.
A mystery. A secret. A truth that brings true transformation. This
has been a crisscrossed journey as I have sought to comprehend
the fuller meaning of the cross and receive this by faith. After all,
I was thoroughly entrenched in dog theology—bad dog, good
dog—both of which lived in me and fought constantly to gain
control over my nature. I had a new nature and a new heart, my
teachers said, but my sinful nature remained. My sinful nature
demanded I lust, lie and live recklessly. Stony heart right along-
side the fresh one of flesh. Two-hearted, two-faced monster I
was. Both sinner and saint. And unbeknownst to me, I was a de-
spiser of the marvelous grace of God—the grace demonstrated
by Jesus on the cross, the cross where I, too, was crucified with
Christ. I had much to learn. And I was oh-so hungry.

I was hungry to be all Jesus wanted me to be. I was achingly
aware of how far I fell short of His description of a true disciple.
My inventory of sins haunted me. If only I could finally pick

up my cross, crucify myself and die. If only I could discipline myself enough to suppress the old, selfish me. I knew if I just tried harder, things would improve. And they often did, for a while anyway. But my old habits would catch up with me and there I was again, in the slough of despair. Eating too much chocolate. Dreading prayer time at church. Wanting to watch a romance movie rather than read my Bible. Losing patience with my whiny two-year-old. Not wanting to have sex with my husband because I was so tired from homeschooling children all day. Ignoring the call from my needy neighbor. I was really a pathetic Christian. What must I do to be changed for good?

The report of the amazing revival in another part of the world got my attention. Many lives were transformed. These people were living as victorious disciples of Jesus. What was their secret? The article revealed what I had to do: Make a detailed list of every sin in my life. Do not hold back. List everything. After the list was complete, I was to repent with as much sorrow as I could muster. Then, I should make a bold determination to kill off these sins with reinvigorated discipline and voila, transformation would come. Except, it did not. Oh, sure. There was some change. Willpower and determination can produce some behavior modification. But there was no true transformation. I was just a sinner, saved by grace—with unsuccessful attempts to sustain change by woeful self-effort. Sin management failed again. "Saint Dianne" was a delusion . . . or was she?

Burning Questions

In my weakness, He is strong. His grace is truly sufficient (see 2 Corinthians 12:9). But the stronghold of sin has been dismantled. I do not have to continue to live one moment longer submitted to sin's power. Our union assures me of His love that never fails and His presence that never leaves. I am no longer a sinner. I am a saint. I love the Romans 6:6 footnote in *The Passion Translation*: "To beg God for victory over sin is a refusal to understand that we have already died to sin. Our joyful task is to believe the good news, rather than to seek to crucify ourselves. Sin is not suppressed by the cross; it is eliminated."[4] Believing this has massive ramifications for our lives. For one, we stop trying to fix the old me. Yet for many believers, questions remain.

Do You "Confess" Your Sin?

Yes, if you mean talking with Jesus about this breach in our relationship, this damage to our union. I talk with Him and let Him know I need His help to live as a saint. If you mean confessing to "get forgiveness," then the answer is no. I already have forgiveness. Jesus gave that to me based on His work on the cross, not my work of confessing. The difference is significant. There is a choice. But this is not a choice to buck up, suck up and power through a temptation. That is often done apart from Jesus and not in union with Him. He is not waiting for me to get all my ducks in a row. He is not watching me from afar to see if I can figure out how to deal with the current crisis or conundrum. No, He is inside of me. He provides all I need to live in the reality of my new creation—my holy, clean, righteous life as a saint now and a sinner no more. I rest in that and receive His help.

What about Christians Who Commit Suicide?

When a young teenager (I will call him Scott) in our church family tragically committed suicide, some people were convinced he was doomed to hell even though he had been an active believer in Jesus. When questioned, they responded that Scott did not have the chance to confess the sin of taking his own life and therefore could not be forgiven and thus he was lost forever. This lie is almost as tragic as the suicide. Scott's salvation did not depend on his making sure every sin was confessed before he died. Scott's salvation, and ours, too, is based solely on our faith in Jesus and His work on the cross—a work that grants us forgiveness for all our sin—past, present and future—and makes us a new being.

"'I will not ever again remember their sins and lawless deeds!' So if our sins have been forgiven and forgotten, why would we ever need to offer another sacrifice for sin?" (Hebrews 10:17–18 TPT).

No more sacrifice for sin. Scott was safe with Jesus. Does this mean we just live recklessly, indulging in all kinds of sin since we know all sins are forgiven? That is crazy! If we are in union with the sinless One who destroyed sin, we do not continue in sin. Period.

"And you know without a doubt that Jesus was revealed to eradicate sins, and there is no sin in him. Anyone who continues to live in union with him will not sin" (1 John 3:5 TPT).

We live in union with Jesus. He is in us. Normal behavior is *no sin*. If I do sin—get angry at my husband, lie about a friend, overindulge at the party—I try to be quick to let Jesus know that is not how I want our relationship to be. I am sorry for my sin. I want to reflect His image, His character and His victory over sin in all my life. I want to live in a way that honors His total sacrifice for sin, a sacrifice that took away my sin.

How Can I Overcome Temptation?

David (not his real name) is a handsome, fun-loving twenty-something who leads a great small group of young adults at our church. My grandkids adore him, especially when he joins in their water balloon fights in our backyard pool. They fondly refer to him as "Uncle David" and beg for me to include him at our large family gatherings, and of course I do. He is a committed Christian, hardworking employee and all-around stellar guy. I consider him another son in our family and love him in that way.

David told us this year that he is gay. He has tried to deny it, control it, change it, but he continues to have a strong attraction to other men. He knows that we believe God's will is heterosexuality. He confessed his sexuality struggle to us with humility and fear. I am still processing David's confession, loving him as always and asking Jesus how to respond. There is not a "quick fix" or an easy compromise. This is a sensitive, real dilemma, a touchy tension. I know that Jesus, who lives inside each of us, was truly tempted in every way and is ready to help us in every situation.

> This is why he had to be a Man and take hold of our humanity in every way. He made us his brothers and sisters and became our merciful and faithful King-Priest before God; as the One who removed our sins to make us one with him. He suffered and endured every test and temptation, so that he can help us every time we pass through the ordeals of life.
>
> Hebrews 2:17–18 TPT

Jesus endured every temptation so He can help us.

One day He said to me, *Did you know I was tempted to have a homosexual relationship?*

What?

Yes, He continued, *I lived with twelve men.*

Jesus was tempted in every way. This is not just a glib state-ment to make us feel better. He was tempted to hate, lust, be proud and be jealous. Living in union to overcome these tempta-tions is a radical dependence on Christ in us who overcame them all. It is not us doing it on our own while He watches from afar saying, *I did it. You can, too!* He is in us, supplying all we need to walk in righteousness. This is radical. This is revolutionary. This is the righteousness of God in Christ.

We truly can do nothing apart from Him. Overcoming sin, overcoming temptation or dealing with any sort of internal battle must be done in union with Jesus, with God as our source.

> Everyone who is truly God's child will refuse to keep sinning because God's seed remains within him, and he is unable to continue sinning because he has been fathered by God himself. Here is how God's children can be clearly distinguished from the children of the Evil One. Anyone who does not demonstrate righteousness and show love to fellow believers is not living with God as his source.
>
> 1 John 3:9–10 TPT

When we first learned this sinner/saint message, I felt a heavy burden at times. I thought I had to remember who I was in Christ as a righteous saint, renew my mind to my resurrected self through Scripture, choose daily to live in this truth and overcome all temptation that came my way. I was drowning again, under responsibility. I was not able to respond to Jesus in me with uncomplicated trust, love and peace. It felt again like a performance, except it was a more difficult performance than when I had a sinner identity and lots of excuses for failure. I knew the Holy Spirit was in me, but I was not sure how to rest and respond to His empowering of me to be a saint. I share this to encourage you to stay sensitive to His gentle instruction and generous help. He is committed to our union being healthy and our transformation being true.

It does take a choice to live in this transforming truth, which can take time. Forgiveness is often at the core of our living no longer as a sinner, but as a saint. Forgiveness is, after all, the core message of the cross. That does not mean it is easy or that it really makes sense.

How Can I Forgive Others?

Claire (not her actual name) adored her Italian grandparents. When her family's finances failed, they moved into the grandparents' spacious home for a season. Consuming mounds of delicious meatballs and ravioli, dancing to the constant music that filled the corridors, swimming in the huge backyard pool and listening to intriguing stories of faraway Italy made for a fairy-tale life for Claire and her siblings. Of course, it was punctuated by weekly attendance at the beautiful Catholic cathedral, where Claire partook of her first communion and knelt in reverence to the God of her grandparents.

But there was a dark side. The grandfather she loved, trusted and adored insisted that Claire sit on his lap while he worked at his desk. It was during these times that he also worked his hands in places on her body while his body hardened with forbidden pleasure. Claire was confused by the unusual sensations she felt and the sense that something was horribly wrong. Years later, when she finally was able to acknowledge the abuse,

Claire asked, "How does one forgive such a heinous crime, such a horrific sin and such confusing betrayal?" She knew the only Way was Jesus.

This is not a new scenario in our culture where beloved priests, trusted scoutmasters, revered coaches, teachers and uncles have so shamefully violated both boys and girls alike. The trauma is real. The wounds are painful. The memories are seemingly immovable and the ugliness utterly unforgivable. Except, Jesus is clear: "If you forgive those who sin against you, your heavenly Father will forgive you. But if you refuse to forgive others, your Father will not forgive your sins" (Matthew 6:14–15 NLT).

Through hours of counseling others and my own personal experience, I know it is wrong to tell someone to "just choose to forgive." Yes, choice is involved, but first and foremost, we must choose to receive the healing that we need from being so horribly sinned against, then choose to receive the gift of forgiveness that the Father wants to give. This gift often must be received for oneself as self-hatred, guilt and condemnation make for an ugly mix of self-loathing and unforgiveness toward oneself for somehow inviting or tolerating the abuse. It is all so twisted.

The Father wants to make sure we know we are deeply loved, forgiven, accepted and adored as His child. He also wants to empower us to turn and forgive those who have sinned against us. The One who hung on the cross and said, "Father forgive them, they know not what they do," is the same One who lives in each of us. He empowers us to forgive the most unforgivable people. It is miraculous.

While studying Jesus' prayer on the cross, I discovered a fascinating fact about forgiveness. In *The Passion Translation* footnote of Luke 23:34, the translator wrote: "The Greek text implies a repetitive action. . . . As the centurion . . . tied his arms to the crossbeam, Jesus prayed, 'Father, forgive them.' When the spikes tore through each quivering palm, he prayed again, 'Father, forgive them.' . . . Only heaven knows how many times that prayer was spoken."[5]

Father, forgive them. We may need to pray that prayer over and over. Sometimes for the same people. Sometimes for the same sins done against us. "Jesus, You who live in us, empower us to forgive as You have forgiven. Apart from You, we truly can do nothing, least of all live as the saints You have so miraculously made us to be." Sinners saved by grace. Saints saturated with grace to live in union with Him. Saints now, sinners no more.

--------- **Why Does This Matter?** ---------

Who we think we are determines how we live our life. If we think we are just a "sinner saved by grace," we will still struggle to overcome sin and will live under a cloud of condemnation, in the grip of guilt and the shadow of shame. But worse, as "saved sinners," we live in sorrowful contempt of the cross and Jesus' tremendous sacrifice. It is that serious.

--------- **What Can I Do Right Now?** ---------

Abandon any twisted theology of two natures. Ask the Holy Spirit to lead you into the truth of the cross and your new identity as a saint. Stop trying to fix the old you. No more makeup

101

on your corpse! Trust your union with Jesus as you learn to live as a new creation with a new heart.

Thank You, Jesus, for taking us to the cross and into the tomb and raising us up with Your righteousness to live as saints now, sinners no more. Empower me to grow and live in this incredible reality.

Better Drunk Than Sober

Jesus provides the best wine. Get drunk daily in the Holy Spirit and enjoy life with Him. God created us for the enjoyment of many pleasures with Him.

BUT DOESN'T THAT MEAN I'LL LOOK FOOLISH? WHAT ABOUT REASON? PLUS, I FEEL GUILTY ENJOYING ORDINARY PLEASURES!

Thousands of students dressed in green staggered into the streets, shouting, slurring their words and stumbling all over one another while balancing paper cups foaming with beer as part of "Unofficial," an annual St. Patrick's Day celebration where huge numbers of usually sober-minded undergrads engage in all-day drunken decadence. For over 25 years, this infamous event has taken place on the campus of the University of Illinois at Champaign-Urbana—a world-renowned research institution with a reputation for groundbreaking discoveries in computer technology, engineering and the sciences. In this university town, where I have lived for over fifty years, science is supreme, the mind is most important and reason rules. Better sober than drunk here any day, except "Unofficial," of course. So ironic!

I am a proud graduate of the University of Illinois and an avid learner and lover of all things that challenge the mind. It is no secret, however, that reason can become the enemy of revelation and that science can strangle the Spirit. Since our God, the Creator of the universe, is by far the smartest being in that universe and the actual brilliance behind our brains, there should be no contention between an experiential faith and a faith grounded in facts and figures.

We, as believers, are designed to be drunk in the Spirit (see Acts 2:12–15) as well as "watchful" and "sober-minded" (1 Peter 5:8). Both drunk and sober. But if I had to choose, I believe God says, *Better drunk than sober!*

Jesus made that clear in John 7:37–38 (TPT): "All you thirsty ones, come to me! Come to me and drink! Believe in me so that rivers of living water will burst out from within you, flowing from your innermost being, just like the Scripture says!" At that moment, "Jesus was prophesying about the Holy Spirit that believers were being prepared to receive. But the Holy Spirit had not yet been poured out upon them, because Jesus had not yet been unveiled in his full splendor" (verse 39 TPT).

Better to be drunk than sober when it comes to the Spirit.

Why is that? The Holy Spirit is a nonnegotiable for a life in union with Christ. We have a Trinitarian God, and together, this one God has redeemed us and made us a fit home for Himself. The Holy Spirit comes to live inside us as the Father's gift to the Son whom He so graciously poured out on Pentecost. That day, Peter preached:

"God raised Jesus from the dead, and we are all witnesses of this. Now he is exalted to the place of highest honor in heaven, at God's right hand. And the Father, as he had promised, gave him the Holy Spirit to pour out upon us, just as you see and hear today."

Acts 2:32–33 NLT

The Spirit is seen and heard. He is not silent. He is not still. This is not something—or Someone—to be feared, but instead He should be welcomed. Without the Holy Spirit's acknowledged and welcomed presence on a daily basis, no one can live the life our God has prepared for us *now*—this life of glorious, joy-filled union where we experience the Spirit's love and power every day. The Spirit is a marvelous mystery. This means we have to be open to a worldview that involves the miraculous, the unexplainable and, at times, the uncontrollable. That can be hard for those who are skeptical about such experiences, cautious about emotionalism and wary of spiritual drunkenness—and for those who value knowledge, understanding and proof. That is all legitimate, but it is also limiting.

A rational worldview eliminates the possibility of real spiritual interactions with a God whose Spirit blows where He wills and who reveals things our minds cannot access any other way but His way, which is the way of the Spirit. As Paul wrote:

"No eye has seen, no ear has heard, and no mind has imagined what God has prepared for those who love him." But it was to us that God revealed these things by his Spirit. For his Spirit searches out everything and shows us God's deep secrets. No one can know a person's thoughts except that person's own spirit, and no one can know God's thoughts except God's own

Spirit. And we have received God's Spirit (not the world's spirit), so we can know the wonderful things God has freely given us.

1 Corinthians 2:9–12 NLT

The Spirit has now been poured out! Are you thirsty for a more experiential, overcoming, transformed life as a follower of Jesus? Do you want to live in union with the Triune God—Father, Son and Holy Spirit? It is as simple as saying, "Jesus, I believe You. I want You to fill me with Your Spirit," and then expect to feel His presence bubbling up within you or upon you. If you open your mouth, you may speak forth in a unknown language, just as the disciples "were all filled and equipped with the Holy Spirit and were inspired to speak in tongues—empowered by the Spirit to speak in languages they had never learned" at Pentecost (Acts 2:4 TPT).

For those who have questions, I have written more extensively on the different phenomena of the Holy Spirit in my book *Hello, Holy Spirit: God's Gift of Live-in Help* (CreateSpace, 2017). The one thing I want you to grasp is the importance of being initially baptized in (with) the Holy Spirit and the desire to be filled again and again. Paul exhorted the early believers: "Don't drink too much wine. That cheapens your life. Drink the Spirit of God, huge draughts of him" (Ephesians 5:18 MSG).

The Spirit Is Not Deceased

Just as a university is rooted in reason (and rightly so), much of religion is also rooted in reason. But that can be wrongly so. Reason can relegate the Spirit to a stiff, lifeless concept. I knew that Spirit suffocation well from my youth and was reminded of it when I returned home to my childhood church in March 2020. I sat surrounded by a sea of sober faces staring straight ahead as we listened to the serious tone of the gray-haired pastor. During this somber event, my 93-year-old mother's funeral, I was reminded of thousands of hours I had spent sitting in the same wooden pew filled with the same worn King James Bibles and the same archaic hymnals. I flashed back to falling asleep to the hypnotizing drone of Sunday sermons, sermons that were eerily similar to eulogies shared at funerals like my mother's.

I was struck by the sharp contrast of my strict, sober religious past and my ecstatic, Spirit-filled, dare I say, drunken, present. That is exactly what God says through Luke as He relates how the disciples appeared on Pentecost when the Spirit was poured out:

> "They're speaking our languages, describing God's mighty works!"
>
> Their heads were spinning; they couldn't make head or tail of any of it. They talked back and forth, confused: "What's going on here?"
>
> Others joked, "They're drunk on cheap wine."
>
> That's when Peter stood up and, backed by the other eleven, spoke out with bold urgency: "Fellow Jews, all of you who are visiting Jerusalem, listen carefully and get this story straight. These people aren't drunk as some of you suspect. They haven't had time to get drunk—it's only nine o'clock in the morning. This is what the prophet Joel announced would happen:
>
> "'In the Last Days,' God says, 'I will pour out my Spirit on every kind of people.'"
>
> Acts 2:11–17 MSG

They were not drunk with new wine as some had suspected, but were indeed drunk with new wine of the Holy Spirit. The Spirit loves to fill us with His presence, and this is rarely imperceptible or calm. Others will see and hear. We may feel and speak. We may appear drunk. Drunk with joy. Drunk with power. Drunk with the Living God. Should we expect anything less? After all, He is God, and if He filled us with His presence, we would not only feel something, but others would also perceive that our whole being is touched, even inebriated. *Better drunk than sober!*

Not all agree. If church history is any indication, many disagree, vehemently. So much division, disagreement and downright deception have surrounded the Person of the Holy Spirit. Yes, He is a Person. He is not a power. He is not a principle. He is not a force or a phantom. The Spirit is God and He is in union with us, providing us with His gifts to give away to others in need and working to powerfully transform our own lives. This has not ceased. This has not changed since the first century, but it has been challenged over and over.

Also at my mother's funeral, my somewhat crazy, anticharismatic 85-year-old uncle stopped his wheelchair to talk with me and announced, "Two weeks ago I was baptized in the Holy Ghost! Oh, how I regret my many years of not really knowing Him!" My uncle felt safe sharing such sensational news with me in the stifling atmosphere of a sober church. I was thrilled and I rejoiced with him. Then, a long-lost cousin whom I had not seen for over twenty years grabbed me and relayed one supernatural experience after another, all of which could easily qualify him for immediate excommunication from his conservative church. But he was eager to tell me (I guess the word was out about my drunken Spirit life). He was so thirsty.

I was both dumbfounded and delighted, because the faith in which I was raised is a cessationist faith. Cessationists believe that all gifts of the Holy Spirit (see 1 Corinthians 12:1–11), which were abundantly present in the first century, have now ceased. No speaking in tongues, no miraculous healings, no words from God (i.e., no active, powerful Spirit today). The Holy Spirit may as well be deceased. Yet, He is very much alive. In all fairness, cessationists do believe in the Spirit. They, of course, have the Spirit within, or a new birth would not have occurred (see John 3:5–6). The Holy Spirit is routinely quenched, resisted or ignored. How tragic! This is where many Western churches stand today. Around the world, however, there are over eight hundred million Christians who believe in and practice the gifts of the Holy Spirit and have experienced the Holy Spirit's filling and are labeled charismatic. Charismatics are those who embrace the *charismata*, the gifts of the Spirit.

Why do some continue to live blinded to the truth and hence bereft of the exhilarating experience of Holy Spirit baptism or infilling? What has kept good, faithful, godly people sober when they could be drinking great draughts of the Spirit? Is it reason? Fear? Ignorance? Unworthiness? Religion? I do know the Spirit is on the move, visiting those who are hungry. The Spirit is inviting people to be baptized—soaked—in Him.

Brain Power

While my whole being has been transformed, I am especially grateful for the impact of the Spirit on my mind. Receiving the Holy Spirit and allowing Him to become my Teacher has brought so much freedom, growth, stability and memory help, too. Jesus said: "But when the Father sends the Spirit of Holiness,

109

the One like me who sets you free, he will teach you all things in my name. And he will inspire you to remember every word that I've told you" (John 14:26 TPT).

We have the most brilliant Being in the universe as our Teacher, and He lives inside us. That is a real brain boost. In our union as Teacher and student, however, there is no magical mind transformation or brain dump of divine wisdom. There is an ongoing school of the Spirit where He adjusts our beliefs, exposes lies, reveals new things, leads us into all truth and brings things to our remembrance. Why not include the expertise of the Holy Spirit in all you do—work, play, rest and study? This seems like a no-brainer (no pun intended), but this practice of mentally living in union with the Spirit does require a major shift in one's worldview. You have to be open to other realms than the one you can see and control. You have to have eyes that see.

Privately, Jesus told His disciples, "Blessed are the eyes that see what you see! For I tell you that many prophets and kings desired to see what you see, and did not see it, and to hear what you hear, and did not hear it" (Luke 10:23–24).

Years ago, I was enslaved to logic and saw only with my physical eyes, especially in regard to things of God. Then, I was shown a different lens that rattled my cage of reason and exposed a flaw in my perspective. I was introduced to the work of the late Paul Hiebert, who was a distinguished professor of mission and anthropology at Trinity Evangelical Divinity School and leading missiological anthropologist before his death in 2007. Hiebert was best known for his concept of the "excluded middle."

He believed that most of us in the Western hemisphere see the universe as consisting of two tiers—the invisible things of the heavenly world and the visible things of this earthly world. Because of this perspective, we Westerners exclude the part in between or in the middle, hence the term "excluded middle." Here in the excluded middle are the invisible things of this world, and in particular the unseen personal beings, such as angels and demons. Hiebert suggested that non-Westerners are much more likely to accept this "excluded middle" and the reality of demons and angels and other spiritual beings. This perspective makes a big difference in the way people approach life's problems, including disease.

In an article entitled "The Flaw of the Excluded Middle," Hiebert shared about his experience as a Western missionary in India. India is a country where the middle is *not* excluded, and thus, the reality of demons, ancestors and spiritual forces play a large part in treating disease and managing life. This is in contrast to an excluded middle view that only addresses sickness and life from a scientific, medical paradigm. Concerning his experience in an Indian village, Hiebert wrote this:

> John's disciples asked, "Are you he that should come, or do we look for another?" (Luke 7:20). Jesus answered not with logical proofs, but by a demonstration of power in the curing of the sick and casting out evil spirits. So much is clear. Yet when I read the passage as a missionary in India, and sought to apply it to missions in our day, I had a sense of uneasiness. As a Westerner, I was used to presenting Christ on the basis of rational arguments, not by evidence of his power in the lives of people who were sick, possessed and destitute. In particular, the confrontation with spirits that appeared so natural a part of Christ's ministry belonged in my mind to a separate world of the miraculous—far from ordinary everyday experience.[1]

Hiebert wondered if his uneasiness was due in part to his own worldview that excluded the middle level of the supernatural. As a scientist he had been trained to deal with the empirical world in naturalistic terms. As a theologian, he was taught to answer ultimate questions in theistic terms. The middle zone did not really exist for him. Unlike Indian villagers, he had given little thought to spirits of this world, to local ancestors and ghosts, or to the souls of animals. Hiebert and other missionaries trained in the West had no answers to the problems of the middle level because they often did not even see it. When tribal people spoke of fear of evil spirits, Western missionaries denied the existence of the spirits rather than claim the power of Christ over them.

After a time of Scripture study, soul searching and experiencing life on the mission field, Hiebert knew it was wrong to deny the existence of this spiritual realm. His view was flawed. He humbly embraced the "excluded middle" and went on to impact thousands with his subsequent writing and teaching. He brought excellent, sober scholarship to the importance of this revelation and drew others into the liberating power of the Spirit. His work changed the way I approached ministry, but it also upended the way I did life.

Dualism versus Incarnation

Anticipation rippled through the packed sanctuary when our church launched a new sermon series titled "Money, Sex, Power, Beer!" These messages garnered far more interest than any others our team had preached in the previous thirty-plus years. Why? This is where we live—the real world of stressful finances, unsatisfactory sex, lust for influence and, last but not least, the tempting escape via the numbing pleasures of alcohol. But the divide is wide and the tension is taut in many of our dualistic Christian lives: spiritual versus secular, holy versus profane, sacred versus sinful, no versus yes. Even those who have embraced the Spirit tend to exclude Him from everyday life— where we work, make love or enjoy a beer with our neighbor. Unleashing our restrained pleasure in His presence can feel unholy.

God created humans to live in a garden called Eden, which literally means "pleasure."[2] In this beautiful place, filled with His presence, Adam and Eve enjoyed His companionship, along with His glorious creation. One of His first instructions to them was to "be fruitful and multiply" (Genesis 1:28)—an obvious encouragement to delight in the sexual intimacy He designed. His will for us as His children, therefore, is pleasure, not prudishness nor perverted passion.

In each of us, made in God's image, is the longing to drink deeply of those streams of pleasure that flow from His side, not those from the world's polluted waters or from religion's prudish trickles. The psalmist wrote, "I long to drink of you, O God, drinking deeply from the streams of pleasure flowing from your presence" (Psalm 42:1 TPT).

God loves to lavish His good things on us, bringing us pleasure. "Trust instead in the one who has lavished upon us all good things, fulfilling our every need" (1 Timothy 6:17 TPT).[3]

If this is so, why is there so much angst?

At the root of much of our misunderstanding is the Greek dualism that has shaped many of our ideas about theology, science, politics, religion and life itself. *Come out and be separate!* cries the voice of religion. Dualism does crazy things, distorting God's desire for us to enjoy life here on earth. Better to be sober with uptight spirituality than drunk with our deity's delight—so the thinking goes.

For this discussion, we will use the word *dualism* to simply mean the division into two separate parts—the visible and the invisible, the material and the mental, the natural and the spiritual, God and man—so that there is little overlap or integration of the two. This separation has influenced the practice of our faith as we try to connect with a God who is far off, aloof and not all that happy with our "unspiritual" lifestyle.

From an academic point of view, *dualism* can be a difficult word to define. New Testament scholar, Pauline theologian and Anglican bishop N. T. Wright noted, "In *The New Testament and the People of God* I listed no fewer than ten significantly different uses to which the word 'dualism' was being put within biblical studies, and I pointed out the muddle which this linguistic and conceptual slipperiness has occasioned."[4]

While delineating which definitions of dualism are and are not helpful, he goes on to clarify that the potentially damaging dualism for us as believers is one that makes a sharp divide that hinders our full engagement with God here on earth as His image bearers:

> The radical rejection by most ancient Jews, in particular, of what we find in Plato and in much oriental religion, and the radical embrace of space, time and matter as the good gifts of a good creator God, the place where this God is known and the means by which he is to be worshipped—all this remains foundational, and is firmly restated and underlined in the New Testament.[5]

Dualistic thinking has had an unfortunate influence on Christianity since the first century, and even now many continue to think it is more spiritual to go to church than to go sailing, skiing or shopping. Viewing life from a non-dualistic perspective, however, means that in all we do we are members of the Body of Christ. We are the Church whether we are sailing, skiing or shopping. We are the Church regardless of what we are doing: worshiping, working or walking the dog.

So how did we get so super spiritual that we are of no earthly good? How did we get so enmeshed in a view that excludes the middle and the Spirit's activity in everyday life?

The very Gospel we claim to believe declares that our God, the most spiritual being in the universe, became a human being—the most ordinary, earthly creature in the universe. A union between God and man occurred that set the stage for us to become partakers of the divine nature. This miraculous, mysterious event, known as the incarnation, can radically change us when we allow its magnificent truth to infuse our whole life. Heaven and earth are united. And the Spirit makes this union real in all of life.

As the early Church father Irenaeus so famously said, "Jesus Christ, in His infinite love, has become what we are, in order that He may make us entirely what He is."[6] Jesus' incarnation made it possible for us to now live in union with God. His Spirit moves right into our earthly bodies.

One of the most liberating effects of this truth is the discovery that our God, who now lives in this redeemed human home, enjoys the pleasures of this life—eating, drinking, sex, sports, theater, dancing, shopping and playing poker. He enjoys doing life in union with each of us. He is great at keeping these pleasures healthy and free from the excesses that can tragically turn our pleasure into painful problems. Jesus' experience as a man did ensure that He would be a faithful High Priest, able to help us in all of our temptations, too (see Hebrews 4:14–15). Jesus is likewise ready to help worn-out believers who are weary of sin management and spiritual sobriety.

To Drink or Not to Drink

Author Paul R. Smith had a high value for being serious, studious and sober. Then he saw Ephesians 5:18, "Don't get drunk with wine . . . but be filled by the Spirit" (HCSB), in a new light.

> This had always sounded to me like a nice little moralism, something like, "Don't go to the bar and get loaded. Instead, stay at home and read the Bible." . . . But Paul was quite specific in his advice. Instead of filling up with alcoholic spirits, fill up with God's Spirit. What possible connection is there between getting drunk and being filled with the Spirit? In the experience of the early Christians, there was a whopping big connection. At Pentecost, when the Spirit came upon Jesus' followers en masse, they became so happy they were actually accused of being drunk![7]

Don't drink too much wine. Do get drunk in the Spirit. As you invite the Holy Spirit to fill you, you will discover that the Scripture opens up to you, your conversations with God multiply and your mystical faculties are enhanced. Smith continued:

> In my ardent search for theological understanding, I found that the former dean of the Harvard Divinity School, Krister Stendahl, had written, "Opening up the full spectrum of religious experience and expression is badly needed in those churches that have suppressed the charismatic dimension. Flashlight-battery-voltage Christianity is certainly not strong enough for

fighting the drug habit. And no religious tradition can renew itself without the infusion of raw and fresh primary religious experience."[8]

If we ever needed the power of a personal, loving God, it is now. The Holy Spirit is ready to infuse us with His raw, fresh, liberating presence. Smith concluded: "I had a Master of Divinity in New Testament and theology from a Southern Baptist seminary. . . . Here I was, with a graduate degree called a 'Master of Divinity,' having mastered very little about my divinity!"[9]

Paul Smith's life was radically impacted by his encounter with the Spirit. Better drunk than sober. I detail my own liberation from stuffy sobriety to drunken delight of the Spirit-filled life in *Hello, Holy Spirit*. There is no question that my initial and subsequent baptisms in the Spirit revolutionized my entire life. While I do not have lots of letters after my name and have not been to seminary like Paul Smith, I do identify with the failure of book learning to satisfy my thirst and to align with biblical revelation. I have felt the pressure to get my master of divinity degree. Was it pressure to learn more or pressure to please others whose respect I coveted? What did my Master Himself think?

> Brothers and sisters, consider who you were when God called you to salvation. Not many of you were wise scholars by human standards, nor were many of you in positions of power. Not many of you were considered the elite when you answered God's call. . . . For it is not from man that we draw our life but from God as we are being joined to Jesus, the Anointed One. And now he is our God-given wisdom, our virtue, our holiness, and our redemption.
>
> 1 Corinthians 1:26, 30 TPT

We are in union with Jesus, our Master of Divinity, who is our God-given wisdom. He gladly shares that wisdom with us. Learning is best when done in union with Jesus whether we earn a graduate degree or not because "we have the mind of Christ" (1 Corinthians 2:16).

Enjoying Life in Union

I'm looking forward to our date to see Little Women *at the Village Theater tonight.*

Whose voice was that? My husband was sound asleep in the next room. And I already knew he was not overly excited about spending two and a half hours watching another rendition of Louisa May Alcott's famous treatise on young women. I knew he was doing me a birthday favor by agreeing to my choice of our movie date. Who was looking forward to our date? Then it dawned on me. Jesus. The One who lives in me, the One who is in union with me, let me know that He was quite excited about what we were doing to celebrate my birthday—watching a "chick flick," *Little Women.*

There are many activities that Jesus really enjoys, but we can fail to acknowledge His presence in us as we engage in them. Why is this? For many of us, raised in a dualistic religious culture, we find it hard to adjust to the truth that Jesus enjoys so much of life, real life, including going to the theater.

In my own growing-up years, I endured a long list of "forbidden pleasures": Theaters were evil. Movies were out (both outside and inside our home). And there was no such thing as a VCR, let alone a smart TV, which gave one unlimited access to all kinds of media. But it would not have mattered because I was raised in a home without a television set. Television was

118

considered a pipeline for sewage—spiritual sewage—into one's home and heart. TVs were banned for all members of our church. While it was often embarrassing and humiliating to be the only girl in my gang of friends who could not join the conversations about *The Twilight Zone* or *The Brady Bunch*, it was even worse that the lack of a TV made my home the last place anyone wanted to come for our popular weekend sleepovers. I was so ashamed.

There were definite advantages to not having a TV, although these were overshadowed by my adolescent shame. Years later, I realized my love for *National Geographic* magazines, my devotion to reading books of all kinds and my lifelong enjoyment of Scrabble, Clue and Sorry were all a direct result of no TV in our home. But the lack of a TV unfortunately translated into these beliefs: God hates TV. God hates pleasure. God is so disappointed when we partake in such activities. He is a curmudgeonly God. Because of these beliefs, I left Him out of so much of my life, long after I moved from my TV-less home and was convinced that TV and movies were permissible for a Christian.

I left Him out, not so much in shame, but just because I was totally ignorant of His delight in earthly pleasures and, of course, of His presence in me as I engaged in them. I did much of my life without Him. I spent hours watching great productions oblivious to my union with Christ. I also spent hours watching less than stellar, sometimes altogether stupid shows (who writes these?). I would crawl into bed feeling slimed and even a tad ashamed. Including Jesus in my selection of entertainment, however, brought "refreshment to my bones" (Proverbs 3:78)—and my inner being. Jesus is good at alerting us to bypass certain shows or even turn off the TV. He can be a bit picky about what He wants to watch, and we would do well to heed His advice. But there are many wholesome and stimulating movies that Jesus loves to watch with us.

Once I was on a plane and searched for an enjoyable movie for the long flight. I was frustrated at the plethora of raunchy selections. Then, I saw a movie called *Tolkien* and I recognized the name as that of the author of the famous *The Lord of the Rings* series. I have never read the books or watched the fabulously popular movies because I am not a fan of fantasy. I love a good biography, however, so I clicked on the movie and watched an inspiring story of J. R. R. Tolkien. My eyes welled with tears and I sensed the presence of the Spirit as I watched this movie in union with Jesus.

Jesus is also interested in joining us as we appreciate the artistic efforts of other human beings. My trip to see the *Nutcracker* ballet at Christmastime was an opportunity to be overwhelmed with absolute awe at the talents, effort and beauty of very young children as they performed difficult ballet moves. Jesus within me was excited as together we rejoiced in the human body, masterfully created by Him. We admired those talented adults and children as they used their God-given abilities to float across the stage while the gifted orchestra filled the auditorium with the beloved notes penned by Tchaikovsky years ago. Not only did Jesus and I have a wonderful time observing the ballet, but we also had the privilege of watching five of my young granddaughters be mesmerized by the ballet. Doing life in union with Jesus brings much joy at so many levels.

I am sad that I missed out on much of this while raising our children. I was still trying to get free from dualism and the belief that God is picky about pleasurable activities of any kind. We restricted our children to watch only "godly" or safe

TV shows like *Superbook*, *Gospel Bill* and *Little House on the Prairie*. We did not allow any *Smurfs* or *Scooby-Doo*, as these were "too demonic." This was just one of many parenting mistakes we made, although there was definite merit in monitoring what our children watched. I am now trying to make up for the lost years by tuning in to our union as I interact with all of my grandchildren.

Whether it is boogie boarding in the Atlantic Ocean, skiing down a snow-covered hill in Wisconsin or just reading a favorite scary story around the campfire, I now choose to do all in union with Jesus—and the grandchildren. Jesus loves children, and I have loved experiencing His love—in me—for them as we do life together. Jesus puts the "fun" in dysfunctional family life along with a good dose of laughter and lots of unconditional love for ornery children.

Am I always aware of our union when hanging out with the grandkids?

No. Sometimes I am too tired, too annoyed by their disobedience or too distracted. But the Spirit is faithful to remind me to tune in and taste how good His presence is in me, in children and in the pleasures of life. Once again, I drink great draughts of the Spirit and overflow with joy and thanksgiving.

As Paul wrote to the believers at Colossae, "Let every detail in your lives—words, actions, whatever—be done in the name of the Master, Jesus, thanking God the Father every step of the way" (Colossians 3:17 MSG). Drink huge draughts of the Spirit. The Spirit of God is intoxicating. And we have the choice of whether or not we will drink of Him. This does not mean we walk around falling over all the time. But we are aware that we carry God Himself and that is not boring nor is it "normal" as we may have known in the past.

So choose to do all of life in union with Jesus. Your interests are different from mine. Ask Jesus what He enjoys doing with you. Golfing? Running? Fishing? Woodworking? (Jesus is really an expert here, having been a carpenter on earth.) Painting? Ceramics? Photography? Get ready to be surprised. Include Him in all your daily activities. I have noted how frequently He reminds me of what He enjoys in union with me—working, playing, swimming, cooking, gardening and even shopping.

Jesus loves shopping? That was a big surprise to me.

Isn't that too worldly at its worst or too boring at its best for Jesus?

Jesus has important ministry to do. Yes, and He has time to do ordinary life with me, too. Most of all, He loves to do this in union with us. Even at Kohl's, Field & Stream or Best Buy. I am alert for more things Jesus enjoys in me but that I have often thought were my own initiative or just too ordinary for His extraordinary Spirit to partake.

My joy intersects with the joy of Jesus. I am learning to do everyday life in union with Him—we do not "do" dualism. At first, I am fully immersed in the event at hand, seated at my large wooden dining table laden with good food, listening to the laughter coming from the twelve chairs filled with sons, daughters and grandchildren. There are yellow and pink flowers from my garden, a bowl of delicious-smelling Italian beef, a vibrant veggie tray and a fresh fruit salad piled high with pineapples, strawberries and grapes. Then, a brief nudge catches me, and I realize, *Jesus, You're really enjoying this, aren't You?*

Why is that so surprising? Jesus loves good food. He loves eating with friends. After all, have you noticed how often the Gospel accounts revolve around Jesus eating with others? Jesus enjoyed eating at big picnics, small dinner parties, wine-soaked weddings and solemn Passover feasts. Jesus is a human being who loves good food and drink. Of course, the drink can throw you a bit, if you were taught to avoid alcohol altogether. As with all pleasures, alcohol can easily be abused. But when you enjoy a glass of wine in union with Jesus and your good friends, you truly do taste and see how good He is. And it is best to stop at two glasses. Better sober than drunk.

Why Does This Matter?

Jesus became a human—the God-man—born as a baby, raised in a family, employed in the wood shop, surrounded by good friends, good food and even a bit of fun. He lived all of life in union with the Spirit and wants to do the same in us. Sure, there were plenty of troubles (He was, after all, betrayed, denied, beaten and crucified). But He became what we are in order for us to become what He is and He graciously offers us His Spirit to do all of life together. It gives Him great pleasure to give us His pleasure. Will we resist His Spirit in favor of reason? Will we ignore His presence in favor of prudence? Or will we agree with Him when He says, *Better drunk than sober—with the Spirit, that is!*

What Can I Do Right Now?

Ask Jesus to baptize you in the Holy Spirit, and receive a fresh awareness of His presence in your whole life. Be alert for and welcome Him in the everyday and the extraordinary, the mundane and the miraculous, the silly and the serious. Laugh more, frown less as you daily drink great draughts of the Spirit.

Father, thank You for saturating every part of my being with Your very own Spirit. I welcome You, Holy Spirit, to empower me to reflect Jesus in all I say and do.

— 6 —

Intimacy, Not Imitation

Jesus wants intimacy with you,
not imitation of Him. He wants participation,
not performance.

HOW DO I HAVE INTIMACY WITH AN INVISIBLE GOD?

Hunger pains gnawed at my stomach as I entered my friend's kitchen. I spied the bright orange clementines piled high in a glass bowl in the center of the table and began to salivate at the thought of the fruit's sweetness. We were staying as guests for a few days while the owners were away, and while I would not ordinarily have helped myself to their food, this fruit looked scrumptious. I knew they would not mind, and I was famished from traveling the whole day, so I grabbed the top piece. I expected to feel the familiar squish of the easy-to-peel, textured skin. Instead, my fingers wrapped around a hard, unmovable piece of orange plastic. Surprise and disappointment hit me as I realized that this lovely clementine was not real and certainly not edible.

Imitation fruit—real looking on the outside but real empty on the inside.

Imitation fruit for a Christian is no different. Our feigned joy, peace, love, faith and patience are only a slight poke away from being exposed as counterfeit. For years, I fooled others and I fooled myself. I only wanted to be a real reflection of what the Scripture said a Christian was like: joyful, peaceful, faithful—a fruit-bearing disciple of Jesus. I did not know that the secret of real fruit production was a genuine union with Jesus, the Vine, who alone can produce the fruit on our branch as we abide in Him. I attempted to imitate Jesus, yet I struggled to produce fruit.

Scripture says to "be joyful always,"[1] so I put on a happy face even when raw grief choked my throat or depression darkened my mind. Scripture says I, as a believer, have "peace of mind and heart,"[2] so I pushed my anxiety down into my knotted stomach and willed my pounding heart to be still. Scripture says the disciples were full of faith, so I boldly proclaimed, "I believe" while fear raged in my bones and doubt tore at my confident facade.[3]

Jesus never intended for us to imitate Him by our self-efforts and willful determination. And yet, thousands of voices have exhorted us to be like Jesus, and we attempt to hang the apple of joy or the pear of peace on the fruit tree of our life. Despair and decay are sure to follow. So how do we bear fruit that Jesus says marks us as His true disciples? Jesus said:

"I am the sprouting vine and you're my branches. As you live in union with me as your source, fruitfulness will stream from within you—but when you live separated from me you are powerless. . . . But if you live in life-union with me and if my

126

words live powerfully within you—then you can ask whatever you desire and it will be done. When your lives bear abundant fruit, you demonstrate that you are my mature disciples who glorify my Father!"

John 15:5, 7–8 TPT

Jesus is clear that a fruitful life as His disciple is possible only as we abide or live in union with Him. We are crucified, buried and risen with Him. We believe this. We embrace this. This alone makes possible our union with our Triune God—the Father, Son and Spirit. Out of this living union we bear much fruit and demonstrate we are mature disciples who glorify our Father. We are not trying to make it happen. While it is an accomplished fact in our Father's heart, we face problems and pressures as the Spirit works it out in our lives. And that is not always pleasant.

WWJD

Hundreds of rowdy teenagers crowded into the church auditorium. Many had been coerced by their anxious parents, who hoped this pre-prom gathering would arm these vulnerable adolescents with the motivation to make wise choices on a night when so many things could go awry. The speaker finished his rousing talk and then displayed the one thing he promised would empower the Christian youth to "flee temptation"—the temptation to drink the purple passion (grape juice and lots of vodka), the temptation to let your hands fall a bit too low while dancing, the temptation to take just one puff of the forbidden pot. What was this powerful tool of prevention? What could possibly harness the hormones of a sixteen-year-old? None other than the WWJD bracelet. Just slip this on your wrist, and when you are tempted, look at the letters and whisper, "What Would Jesus Do?" and poof, you will overcome the temptation to make that sinful choice. Not!

While this was a popular movement in the 1990s, complete with bracelets, posters and T-shirts emblazoned with *WWJD* (my teens had quite the collection, thanks to this anxious parent), it failed to deliver on its promise to empower teens and adults alike to do what Jesus would do. Just knowing what Jesus would do in any given situation does not endue you with power to do it. That was never Jesus' intention, although preachers through the centuries have urged us to "imitate Christ" or "do what Jesus would do." Imitation of Christ has been one false premise that has discouraged the faith of devout believers throughout church history.

Those who want to obey Jesus, love like Jesus and live as He instructs have succumbed to the tyranny and, dare I say, tragic consequences of trying to imitate Christ. Attempted imitation equals failure and frustration. Jesus did not suffer, die and defeat death and the devil so we can now attempt to imitate Him with a bit of willpower. Jesus finished all the work that needed to be done in order to provide us with something far better than an example to follow or a template to try. Jesus invites us into actual participation with Him, into union with Him where His life infuses ours, and together we not only overcome temptation, but we also enjoy a full and abundant life.

The apostle Peter, once an untrained, brash, Christ-denying fisherman, became a man filled with divine life and devotion—the man who, with boldness, would lead the new breed of Spirit-empowered believers, Christ's Church. Peter told us the secret behind such transformation:

Everything we could ever need for life and complete devotion to God has already been deposited in us by his divine power. For all this was lavished upon us through the rich experience of knowing him who has called us by name and invited us to come to him through a glorious manifestation of his goodness. As a result of this, he has given you magnificent promises that are beyond all price, so that through the power of these tremendous promises you can experience partnership with the divine nature, by which you have escaped the corrupt desires that are of the world.

2 Peter 1:3–4 TPT

We have everything we need. These promises offer true transformation and escape from corrupt desires. We can live our entire life in participation with Christ. This is far different from living a life of attempted imitation or strenuous willpower. Participation in the life of Christ brings genuine fruit into our lives—righteousness, peace and joy in the Holy Spirit. We get to experience partnership with the divine nature. That was the Father's plan all along. Jesus is not just an example for us—He "dwelt among us" and would live in us, empowering us to live as He lived.[4] Through our union with Him, we bear much fruit, fruit whose origin is in Him. That bountiful fruit flows out of our union with Christ, not out of our efforts to be like Jesus.

So what about Paul's admonition, "Be imitators of me, as I am of Christ" (1 Corinthians 1:11)? Commenting on this passage, Michael J. Gorman writes:

One of the great Christian spiritual practices is the "imitation of Christ." Despite its popularity, this notion is somewhat at odds with Paul's own spirituality. This claim may sound surprising,

129

since Paul himself says. . . . "Be imitators of me, as I am of Christ." Actually, the verb "be" is "become" . . . which implies a transformative process. More importantly . . . transformation takes place in Christ by the working of the Spirit. [5]

According to Gorman, who has spent years researching this much-debated topic, "at the center of Paul's spirituality of participation and transformation is his notion of mutual indwelling—that is, Christ in believers and believers in Christ."[6] After examining many biblical texts, he concluded cruciformity/theoformity (our union with Christ) is not a question of "imitation but of transformative participation: being in the Messiah/the Spirit and having the Messiah/the Spirit within (mutual indwelling)."[7]

We should expect transformation that comes from real-life participation in the divine nature. This transformation is not merely our own efforts to imitate Christ, but a mutual indwelling of participation. Self-effort results in frustration. Self-effort fuels failure. Self-effort yields fake fruit, and no one wants that.

Jesus Is Our Peace

As the clock crept toward midnight, sleep eluded me. The familiar fear pressed on my chest as my mind filled with dark visions of my sixteen-year-old son's disobedience. Would he violate his curfew again? Would he stumble in smelling of stale smoke and cheap perfume? Would he ignore the questions I leveled—leveled with an anger that obscured the relief I felt when he was home safe at last? Anger that also hid the intense love I had for this troubled teen.

Sirens simultaneously pierced the dark silence of night and the turmoil in my head. New nightmares of mangled cars and drunken teens tormented me. I cried out to Jesus, pleading for Him to send His peace. I was weary with worry and ashamed at the absence of any faith. Indeed, there was no fruit of peace, no fruit of faith and certainly no fruit of biblical parenting in my life.

What kind of Christian are you? taunted the voice in my ear. *Not only have you failed as a parent, but you can't even obey Jesus' command not to worry or be afraid.*

This was the voice of Satan, the accuser. I knew that. The accuser always includes some truth in his attacks. But I agreed with him because I knew Truth lived in me and He would set me free.

Jesus did not answer my desperate pleas for an infusion of fruit that night. He had something far better for me. Jesus had a lesson in fruit bearing that changed my life. It is tempting to think Jesus is going to drop peace, joy, love, patience into our hearts as we cry out. This is a paradigm of separation, not union, and it puts the focus on self, not our Savior.

We cry out, we wait, we persevere, we plead—we, we, we—all the way home. Meanwhile we are filled with condemnation, guilt and shame for our inability to bear the fruit that good Christians bear. Or we can choose to rest in Him and cooperate with what He tells us to do, if necessary. We trust our union with Jesus. Jesus is my Peace. Jesus is my Wisdom. Jesus is my Faith.

I first stumbled on this truth while reading A. B. Simpson, founder of the Christian and Missionary Alliance and one of the most prolific writers about our union with Christ. He not only wrote about our union, he lived it out in every facet of his life. His example deeply impacted my understanding and experience. While he was convinced that his union with Jesus was an accomplished fact through the finished work of Jesus, Simpson knew it was realized through an ongoing relationship in which he learned how to live in union. Here is a brief sample from one of his most famous pieces:

> There came a time when even faith seemed to come between me and Jesus. I thought I should have to work up the faith, so I labored to get the faith. At last I thought I had it; that if I put my whole weight upon it, it would hold. I said, when I thought I had got the faith, "Heal me." I was trusting in myself, in my own heart, in my own faith. I was asking the Lord to do something for me because of something in me, not because of something in Him. So the Lord allowed the devil to try my faith, and the devil devoured it like a roaring lion, and I found myself so broken down that I did not think I had any faith. God allowed it to be taken away until I felt I had none. And then God seemed to speak to me so sweetly, saying, "Never mind, my child, you have nothing. But I am perfect Power, I am perfect Love, I am Faith, I am your Life, I am the preparation for the blessing, and then I am the Blessing, too. I am all within and all without, and all forever.[8]

This truth permeated all of Simpson's life, and out of his intimate union with Jesus, he bore much fruit. But it was always anchored in relationship, a relationship of oneness, love and obedience. Jesus spoke this to His disciples on the eve of His crucifixion.

> "So when that day comes, you will know that I am living in the Father and that you are one with me, for I will be living in you.

Those who truly love me are those who obey my commands. Whoever passionately loves me will be passionately loved by my Father. And I will passionately love you in return and will manifest my life within you."

John 14:20–21 TPT

There is no genuine fruit apart from a union of love. Nature itself (because of Creator God) teaches us this basic reproduction lesson. Our relationship with Christ is pictured as Bride and Bridegroom. This is a marriage union out of which God fulfills His original design for us to "be fruitful and multiply." That command exudes intimacy, passion, union and fruitfulness. Intimate participation is what Jesus wants in our relationship with Him. Intimacy, not imitation. Passion, not performance.

Passion and Our Union

The prophetic atmosphere in the Kansas City warehouse was intoxicating. Thousands of us had spent an hour pouring out our hearts in worship—calling on God to fill us with the Spirit, tears rolling down our cheeks, hands held high and knees bowed low. We were expectant as the popular teacher opened his Bible and encouraged us to be consumed with the same love the Father Himself has for Jesus. This love was the last prayer of Jesus for us (see John 17:26). Would we deny Jesus the answer to His final prayer on earth? We truly wanted passion for Jesus. We wanted to burn with holy fire. We pleaded, repented (again), prayed and praised, and waited to be overwhelmed with passion for Jesus. Some of us even pretended to feel more than we did—an act of faith, we reasoned—as we proclaimed our love for Jesus.

133

But passion for Jesus eluded me much like the beautiful butterfly in my flower garden—so visible, so attractive and then . . . gone. Pursuit of this passion became an obsession. I listened to cartons of cassette teachings, disciplined myself to worship for long stretches and doubled down on my prayer and fasting—all of which were promised paths to this coveted passion for Jesus. This went on for about two years but was complicated by the demands of homeschooling, homemaking and pastoring hundreds of people, too. Then, in January 1990, I decided to talk to Jesus about my failure to have passion for Him. I had highlighted this verse in my Bible: "Grace be with all those who love our Lord Jesus Christ with incorruptible love" (Ephesians 6:24 NASB).

I keyed in on the word *incorruptible* and then proceeded to tell Jesus the many things that could quickly "corrupt" my affection for Him—a bad phone call, a sick child, a cookie binge, a fight with my husband, a body so tired I wore mascara to bed. My list sounded sad and stupid. I did not even mention real problems like poverty, disease, war and racism. I was expecting a good tongue lashing.

Instead, Jesus spoke. *Dianne, I want oneness with you, a union, a marriage. I don't want just a close relationship. I have many friendships. I want oneness. I have passion for you. You want passion for Me, and that is My desire for you. But only My Bride can have true passion for Me. There are no promiscuous lovers allowed. Passion without union is promiscuous. You cannot be a passionate lover of Me without total commitment to Me and absolute faith in Me like a bride and bridegroom. This is a true union with Me, and only our union can produce real passion and abundant fruit.*

He went on to explain that ordinary relationships could not produce genuine fruit, children, as such offspring would be illegitimate fruit and a result of forbidden passion. Pointing to my own marriage to Happy, Jesus said, *You and Hap have much passion, and this union of marriage has produced five fruit—JD, AJ, Julie, J and Cory. But it'd be wrong for you to desire passion for and fruit (children) with Mike, your close friend. That would be lustful passion—producing illegitimate fruit. If you want to experience passionate love for Me, then commit all to Me as in a marriage covenant and trust Me completely.*

In sharp contrast with contemporary culture, Jesus does not want to "hook up" with us, nor is He looking for a "friends with benefits" relationship. He is not interested in cohabitation either, because genuine passion is only released through "marriage"—a total commitment and absolute faith in Jesus (just as in an earthly marriage) for a lifetime union. Jesus had done a good job of courting me before we had this conversation. He had shown me His love and acceptance, brought deep healing of hurts and freed me from the tyranny of religion. I had been an intimate friend with Jesus, but He was inviting me to be His bride and lover.

Always a Bride, Never a Bridesmaid

This experience will be different for each, but Jesus' invitation is the same: *Will you be My bride? Will you enter into union, into oneness with Me with total commitment and absolute faith? If so, our union will be fruitful and you will know true passion.* This intimate language is the language of Scripture: "I will make you my wife forever, showing you righteousness and justice, unfailing love and compassion" (Hosea 2:19 NLT).

Many Scriptures picture our relationship with God, both individually and with others, as an intimate union of bride and Bridegroom, Lover and beloved. Women love knowing they are a beloved bride—always a bride and never a bridesmaid. I took Jesus' invitation seriously. I worked through my personal obstacles so all could be dismantled before I wrote out my absolute surrender and total commitment to our union. Premarital therapy, of sorts, complete with a prenup covenant. I was the one who needed the therapy, not Jesus.

I had quite a few idols that vied for first place in my life—my children and their health, my health, my looks, my marriage, my ministry, my comfort, my security and the list went on. If these were lost or harmed, it would cause me unbearable pain. Could I trust Jesus with all of this? It took some real honest conversations and fresh assurances from the Spirit before I could honestly say "I surrender" with full confidence in Jesus' love and care for me as His wife.

Is this necessary? Can't I just acknowledge the truth and enjoy our union of marriage?

Sure. Each person must engage this truth in a personal way. But I never counsel anyone to rush into marriage without a thorough examination of one's heart. Yes, our union with Jesus is fully accomplished, and we are already "married." But I wanted a true transformation, and I knew there was work to be done in my life. I did not want to just go through the motions of marriage. Dangerous! After months of conversations with the One who loves me unconditionally, lavishly and personally, I signed the covenant I had written, slipped a simple gold band on my finger and drank the wine and ate the bread of my beloved Bridegroom, my Savior, my Lord, my Lover for life with whom I would share the deepest communion forever. Passion flooded my entire being. True fruit was conceived and born with abundant delight.

That ring remains on my finger, a daily reminder of my indissoluble union with my Bridegroom, Jesus. Passion for Jesus remains in my heart, a burning desire to know and love Him more each day. Every time I celebrate communion, I savor the wine and bread as I remember with thanksgiving that because He died and rose—and I with Him—we are in union with one another in this new life as Bridegroom and bride. I now have a clearer revelation of Jesus' words in John 6:56: "The one who eats my body and drinks my blood lives in me and I live in him" (TPT).

He continues to reveal the depth of this truth of Him as our Bridegroom and us as His Bride. One Easter season, I was rereading the account of the crucifixion in the Gospel of John when I came to John 19:30, where Jesus utters the profound words, "It is finished." I have been deeply impacted by this proclamation, which settles our salvation, ushers in our New Covenant and frees us from "trying to get to God." Then, I read this verse in *The Passion Translation* and was stunned when I saw that it read, "It is finished, my bride!" Thankfully there was a footnote. Dr. Simmons, the translator, says that the Hebrew word *kalah* is a homonym that can mean "fulfilled, completed" and "bride."[9] Jesus finished the work of our salvation for us, His Bride. The translation combined both concepts. Jesus continues to work in us to accomplish all that His cross and resurrection have purchased for us, His Bride.

I was overcome with passion and humbled again to realize the price Jesus, my Bridegroom, had paid for me, His bride. Tears flowed freely as I delighted afresh in our union. It is finished. We are forever one as Bridegroom and bride.

Heavenly Intimacy on Earth

Sometimes I stumble on unexpected support for my experience and excitement over our intimate, bride-like union with God. The insights from John Burke's book *Imagine Heaven* inspired me. Burke examined the near-death experiences (NDEs) of thousands and wrote a compelling account about heaven and people's taste of intimacy with God.

> The intimacy of love God has for us is hard to comprehend. . . .
> We can never be as close, as intimate, or as one with another
> person as our souls crave. That is because the oneness we crave
> will only be found when we are united by God with God. God
> likens it to his own marriage to all of us together. . . . Many
> NDErs talk about this oneness they experience in Heaven:
> "Being with Him in heaven, though, made me one with Him in
> a way I could never have imagined. I thought what He thought,
> I dreamed what He dreamed, I felt what He felt." . . . "His love
> is in a different dimension than our idea of love. There is no
> question of his love. . . . We are in him and he is in us. Yet we
> don't lose our identity."[10]

This is what awaits us, but it is also what we can have now. Intimacy must be nurtured, and that is not easy. This is a relationship, not some rigid routine. We must be alert for the tendency to become apathetic or default to the automatic with little anticipation.

"Your Sex Lives Are Pathetic"

I sat at the small desk in the corner of this cozy, cabin-like room and gazed out at the towering emerald pines that hovered close to the glistening lake. Several hundred leaders were gathered for our annual fall retreat at this picturesque camp in the woods of Wisconsin. I was preparing for my evening talk and was waiting for Jesus to give me a fresh word to share with weary men and women who had come for a few days of rest and refreshment. I wanted to encourage these faithful pastors who were always in the giving rather than receiving mode. They certainly did not need another thing to "do." So you can imagine my surprise when I heard these words: *Tell the people, "Your sex lives are pathetic!"*

Was Jesus referring to the common problem we counseled our couples about (i.e., we could not get our unmarried couples to stop having sex and we could not get our married couples to start having more sex)? That might perk up tired ears, but I was not so sure about tired bodies.

Then the Holy Spirit opened my understanding. Jesus was not talking about our physical sex lives. He was referring to our times of intimacy with Him. He went on to say that many of us had lost our first love, our passionate desire to spend time with Him. We no longer "had sex." We no longer spent time just talking tenderly and honestly with Him, worshiping together and delighting intimately with one another. Instead, our time with Jesus was spent preparing for the next Sunday sermon or teaching slot or dutifully sludging through our daily Bible reading and exhausting prayer lists. Pathetic indeed.

I could fully identify. My "sex" life with Jesus had been full of apathy, duty and boredom. Had I replaced delight with duty? I faithfully "did my devotions," but did I express any real devotion to Jesus? I made sure I had "quiet time," but I had to admit it was too quiet—no sweet exchanges of love—just a dry, disciplined reading of my *One Year Bible*. I knew Jesus' tone was not one of chiding or judgment but instead, He was calling us to come: "Come, let's take a break and find a secluded place where you can rest a while" (Mark 6:31 TPT).

What does your secluded place with Jesus look like? How do you rest and reignite intimacy with Jesus?

One day I awoke early and opened my Bible to begin my daily discipline of reading and prayer. Jesus said to me, *I'm bored with your devotions. Let's go swimming!* It was early, the soft golden rays of morning sun were just peeking through the trees, but the July air was already a sultry eighty degrees. Swim, now? Why not? And since that day, I have thoroughly enjoyed many early morning swims in my backyard pool with Jesus. I breathe in His presence, breathe out the cares of the day as my arms churn through the cool, crystal water. The only sounds are the gentle songs of the cardinals and swallows, a soothing contrast to the usual shouts and boisterous laughter of the children who will soon disrupt this intimate moment. In that moment, it is just Jesus and me.

There is no formula, but I know that rest is essential. The One who Himself rested on the seventh day and entreats all His children to take a Sabbath rest really knows that rest is best. Intentionally make time to rest in a way that is most refreshing and replenishing to you. That may not mean lying in your bed or foregoing exercise or embracing ascetic disciplines to quiet your soul. Instead, do those things with Jesus that foster intimacy and rest.

I feel closest to Jesus when we are walking in the bright sunshine and enjoying the beauty of trees draped in a blanket of snow or branches bursting with springtime blossoms. I also draw close to Him while reading—not just the Bible, but a touching memoir of a Holocaust survivor or the biography of a Muslim who miraculously met Jesus. Such stories stir me to love Jesus more than ever. Sipping a hot cup of French roast coffee in front of a roaring fire on an icy Illinois day is a sure way to revitalize our intimacy. No conversation needed. Just the sound of silence as the two of us soak in the warmth of the blaze. Be alert for what Jesus enjoys, too.

Every person is different, but I challenge you to throw off the restraints or rigidity of religion that have inhibited your actual sex lives and do the same in your intimacy with Jesus. There are the common spiritual disciplines that are time-tested ways of growing in intimacy with Jesus—journaling, Bible meditation, prayer, fasting and worship to name a few. Discover what is best for strengthening your intimacy. Discipline does not have to be drudgery or dread. My husband and I find discipline can enhance our lovemaking. When we plan our times of intimacy, we anticipate and prepare to be fully present for one another. No apathy, just ecstasy. But sometimes there is a very real, debilitating intruder on our intimacy.

Who is this "intimacy intruder"?

None other than shame.

Shame on Me!

Oftentimes as believers, we are afraid to live lives of unrestrained passion, thereby bringing shame to our relationship with Jesus, along with a twisted idea of what it means to be a lover—a lover who is assured of absolute acceptance as we abandon ourselves to another. Our shame hides His face from us, inhibits our delight and destroys our "sex lives" with Him. Why is this?

Since 2018 there has been a flurry of articles, books and documentaries that have detailed the failure of the so-called Purity

Movement that was prominent during the same time as WWJD. It went by various names like "True Love Waits" or "Just Say No" or "I Kissed Dating Goodbye." The primary focus was on keeping teenagers and young adults from having premarital sex, or staying "pure" until marriage. Much of the emphasis was directed at the females. They were admonished to dress modestly, to stop seducing young men via sexy appearances, to suppress all shameful sexual desires and to wait until their wedding day for their first kiss. While there were some positive outcomes from this well-intentioned campaign, there was also plenty of damage.

Former evangelical Linda Kay Klein described her search to process the traumatic messages about sex and gender still churning within her in the wake of a shame-based religious upbringing:

> I searched for books, articles, and online communities that might help me understand what I was experiencing. And when I was unable to find any, I called up first one, then two, then several of my childhood girlfriends from my former church youth group. . . . I sat in stunned silence as they told me they were experiencing many of the same things . . . but my struggles continued. Until, at the age of twenty-six, I drove to my midwestern hometown, and set out to find the others.
>
> That year, I began to piece together an epidemic . . . evangelical Christianity's sexual purity movement is traumatizing many girls and maturing women haunted by sexual and gender-based anxiety, fear, and physical experiences that sometimes mimic the symptoms of post-traumatic stress disorder (PTSD). Based on our nightmares, panic attacks, and paranoia, one might think that my childhood friends and I had been to war. And in fact, we had. We went to war with ourselves, our own bodies, and

our own sexual natures, all under the strict commandment of the church.[11]

I have witnessed the war Klein describes. I have prayed with women whose stories are similar to the ones she recounts. It is heartbreaking, and healing is needed. That is where this wonderful gift of intimacy with Jesus is so powerful. Just as shame disrupts and destroys an ordinary, physical sexual relationship, shame has the same effect on our intimacy with Jesus. We are ashamed: ashamed of our past and present sin, ashamed of our inadequacies and insecurities, and ashamed of our nakedness— our inability to be completely honest with a Savior who loves us unconditionally, unlike our human partners.

So what is the solution? Put simply, we are to have faith in the finished work of Jesus and the unconditional love He has for each of us. This solution is the same as it is for every other problem, perversion or pain we have.

Jesus' sacrifice was an unquestioned success in every sense of the word. Jesus bore our shame in the same way that He bore our sin, our sorrow, our sickness, our satanic oppression and our suffering. Jesus took it all on Himself (see Isaiah 53). Jesus does not say, like so many others, *Shame on you!* Because of His willingness to take on our shame, He says, *Shame on Me!* Amazing grace. Astounding love. All available to us now.

The Spirit is ready to expose all the lies that have fed our shame. He wants to wash us with the water of the Word, declaring us beautiful, clean, blameless and loved.

Yet now he has reconciled you to himself through the death of Christ in his physical body. As a result, he has brought you into his own presence, and you are holy and blameless as you stand before him without a single fault. But you must continue to believe this truth and stand firmly in it.

Colossians 1:22–23 NLT

Continue to believe this truth so the Word (and Jesus Himself) can bring you freedom where there is bondage. It does take time. The Spirit leads each one uniquely. But you can stand firmly in faith, be free of shame and delight in your intimacy with Him.

What about Obedience?

"Relationship, not rules. Love, not law," proclaimed the preacher to the crowd of eager listeners. Most were weary of trying to be good, to follow the law, to fully obey God. Many felt like forlorn failures as followers of Jesus. They had tried to obey Jesus' words: "But you are to be perfect, even as your Father in heaven is perfect" (Matthew 5:48 NLT).

But there was always something that tripped them up, and they knew they had disappointed God—again. Love, not law? Relationship, not rules? This new paradigm of faith was attractive, and their attention was fixed as the preacher unpacked the liberating truth of the Gospel. Many of us have been in this crowd of languishing law keepers who finally heard the amazing grace of God made available through the finished work of Jesus. We received the unfailing love of the Father, a fresh, fully forgiven life. We embraced a newfound relational faith not bound by rules or constrained by commandments. We were motivated by passion for God, not by pressure to perform. Ours was a match made in heaven.

But along came the naysayers who accused us of moving from legalism to licentiousness, of sliding down the slippery slope of greasy grace and finally, of being in downright deception and eternal danger. Black/white, either/or paradigms have a way of debilitating our faith. Such perspectives distort the truth. When it comes to our ordinary lives with family and friends, is it a rigid choice of relationship *or* rules? Could it be, and is it not, both/and? All healthy relationships have "rules" per se, but we do not think or act like these dictate our interactions.

For example, I do not say to my adult friends they must abide by "my rule" of not slandering one another. That would be troubling at best and tyrannical at worst. We all know, however, that healthy relationships depend on one another keeping our shared difficulties confidential. We have "rules" that nurture healthy relationships. I do not engage in adulterous liaisons. That would destroy my marriage. Our unspoken "rule" is faithfulness. In the same way, our relationship with God is at its best when we abide by His commands. After all, He is God and He does know what is best for our lives. We can trust His wisdom and His ways. Our obedience is not to get favor with God, but because we already have favor as His much-loved children, bought by the blood of Jesus. His favor causes us to flourish as we live in union with Him.

"For all who obey his commands find their lives joined in union with him, and he lives and flourishes in them. We know and have proof that he constantly lives and flourishes in us, by the Spirit that he has given us" (1 John 3:24 TPT). Ours is a relationship of love. Love of God. Love from God. Love of one another. This is the greatest expression of our union with God. For "God is love" (1 John 4:8, 16).

Delightfully loved ones, if he loved us with such tremendous love, then "loving one another" should be our way of life! No one has ever gazed upon the fullness of God's splendor. But if we love one another, God makes his permanent home in us, and we make our permanent home in him, and his love is brought to its full expression in us. And he has given us his Spirit within us so that we can have the assurance that he lives in us and that we live in him.

1 John 4:11–13 TPT

As we engage in a life of love, we live in the reality of our permanent union with God. Loving others does not make the union happen (Jesus' finished work did that), but it does enhance our experience of living as one with the God who is love. The Spirit within us assures us that God lives in us and we live in Him. This union is strengthened by our practice of receiving His love, loving Him in return and loving others. Through this one big loop of love, we join Him in loving others—by praying for someone, cooking for our family, playing a game with the grandkids, listening to a neighbor or working on a class project. We are aware of His presence, His strength, His love. We walk in intimacy, not imitation. Ours is a oneness of relationship, not rules. Ours is a union of love, not law. We flourish with fruitfulness.

Why Does This Matter?

A life of participation is so much better than the oft-prescribed "imitation of Jesus." Not only do we enjoy passionate love in our union with Jesus, but we are also free from striving. We no longer have to try hard to look like Jesus, act like Jesus, obey like Jesus because Jesus lives in us and through us. We are one—Bride and Bridegroom—ever delighting in one another and participating in all of life together. There is a learning curve, but that is part of the fun of being one. Meanwhile, we can rest in the security of the new covenant, knowing He, unlike so many human spouses, will never leave us. He remains faithful forever.

What Can I Do Right Now?

Have an honest "pour out your heart" conversation with Jesus. Tell Him all the frustrations of your attempts to imitate Him, all your failures to obey His commands and your desire to experience true passion for Him. This is a face-to-face, intimate talk with Jesus. Receive His words of love, affirmation and direction for next steps. He leads one step at a time. Listen to what He has for you so your union with Him can grow deeper and stronger.

Jesus, I love You! Thank You for loving me as Your bride and leading me into a deeper, more fruitful intimacy with You.

— 7 —

Contempt or Compassion?

Jesus asks, "Why do you treat Me with contempt? I desire compassion."

I MIGHT BE TOO COMPASSIONATE OR TOLERANT OF SINFUL BEHAVIOR IN OTHERS. SHOULDN'T I JUDGE WISELY?

The long checkout line at Walmart moved at an even slower than normal pace. I was in my typical hurry and was already late for my lunch appointment. I was annoyed. It was the holiday season, and you would think they would have hired more temporary help. Then I caught a glimpse of the cashier, her dark features obscured by the full scarf around her head. She seemed unfamiliar with the simple tasks of scanning the items as they rolled through on the conveyor platform.

Muslim, I surmised. *Trainee. Poor English. Incompetent.* I seethed with impatience, and I rolled my eyes. I let out a disgusted sigh in hopes of garnering agreement from my fellow line languishers.

Then I heard a voice. *Why do you treat Me with such contempt, Dianne?* I listened again but heard nothing except the faint refrain of "Jingle Bells" and the monotonous ringing of registers. But I knew that voice was Jesus. He sounded stern, but sad, and my heart sank.

I was flooded with conviction and confusion at the same time. Was Jesus saying my contempt for this Muslim woman was contempt for Him? I knew I had made the mistake, again, of failing to see another human being as one made in God's image, of much worth and value. The Holy Spirit had been in the long process of reordering my thinking about all humans, challenging me to view each person with respect, regardless of how messy or in the minority they appeared to be. That had been a long journey of dispensing with my ugly "holier than thou" attitude that reeked of judgement, criticism and condemnation of "sinners." I had finally learned to first see every person as a beautiful human being, made in the image of God. Now, I had regressed and admitted, with sorrow, my failure. But this was a step further.

Why do you treat Me with contempt? Jesus had asked.

How could my treatment of this Muslim cashier be synonymous with my treatment of Jesus? Was Jesus saying He was in her, a Muslim woman? Was Jesus saying He was in union with a person who did not believe in Him as Savior and who even practiced a false religion?

Through all my study to grow in comprehension and experience of union with Christ, I have encountered controversy. This is no topic for the timid. There are land mines of misunderstanding all over and controversies around every corner. The notion that Christ is in all is a current one. Some teach that every human being is already in union with Christ, whether one acknowledges this or is even aware of it. The complexities and nuances of this teaching are many. While I still ponder and pray about that, I do know how important it is to truly love all people, regardless. All human beings are made in the image of God and deserve our respect, even our love.

Jesus' Radical Love

Jesus commands us to love with a radical love: love our literal enemies, love the unlovely homeless, love our annoying workmates, love our rebellious teens, love the incompetent immigrants—love everyone. This is pretty near impossible. Yet Jesus told His disciples, just before His death, "A new commandment I give to you, that you love one another: just as I have loved you, you also are to love one another" (John 13:34).

This Jesus-type love is no soft, sappy sentiment. This radical love is more than a grit-your-teeth tolerance and a forced friendliness. Jesus described His kind of love with a stern challenge:

> "Are you really showing true love by only loving those who love you back? Even those who don't know God will do that. Are you really showing compassion when you do good deeds only to those who do good deeds to you? Even those who don't know God will do that. . . .
>
> "But love your enemies and continue to treat them well. When you lend money, don't despair if you are never paid back, for it is not lost. You will receive a rich reward and you will be known as true children of the Most High God, having his same nature. For your Father is famous for his kindness to heal even the thankless and cruel. Show mercy and compassion for

151

others, just as your heavenly Father overflows with mercy and compassion for all."

Luke 6:32–33, 35–36 TPT

Love my enemies? Lend money to just anyone, even those who I know will not pay back? Overflow with compassion for the cruel? If this was love, I knew that something had to shift in me in order for me to really love people as Jesus loved. He was in me. He knew how to love. I did not. Truth was, I did not know how to love myself. And that is where it had to begin. Jesus instructs us: "You must love your neighbor in the same way you love yourself" (Mark 12:31 TPT).

Love others the same way I love myself. What does that mean, Jesus?

His reply: *Take off your mask. I don't mind your mess. I am a God who looks at you and loves you, mess and all.*

Could that be true? I would have to take a risky step of faith. This is especially difficult for an Enneagram Three. If you are not familiar with this helpful personality tool, grab *The Road Back to You* by Ian Cron, where he delights his readers with descriptions of the nine basic personality types. Each type or number has a distinct way of seeing the world and an underlying motivation that powerfully influences how that type thinks, feels, behaves. In addition, we each have a deadly sin, which Fr. Richard Rohr describes as "the fixations that prevent the energy of life, God's love, from flowing freely. . . . self-erected blockades that cut us off from God and hence from our own authentic potential."[1]

I am an Enneagram Three, which means I am a Performer whose deadly sin is deceit. That sounds horrible. And yet, God

152

looks at me and says He loves me, the real me, and He especially loves it when I choose to remove whatever mask I wear. The mask of the moment depends on the performance of life I am in—mother, pastor, grandmother, counselor, daughter, healer, wife, Christian, prayer warrior, preacher or friend. Having so many roles to perform is exhausting. And so needless. The Father just wants me to be me. He loves me. I can love me, with His love in me.

The Holy Spirit helps you know and love yourself. This is not a license to overlook the dirt on our faces or the warts on our hands. This is a relationship with Jesus where we learn to love our messed-up self and relinquish any excuse for that mess. Until I learned to love my messy self and to receive God's love, I was not able to love all the other messy—and sometimes hard-to-love—people in my world. This love is especially important when it comes to fulfilling the commission Jesus gave us to go into all the world and tell others about Him. Jesus wants to flood us with His compassion and care. But this rarely happens overnight.

Take Off the Judge's Robe

I have always dreaded evangelism. It felt awkward, intrusive, scary. I never liked the models that promoted cold calls. I hated the thought of asking, "If you died tonight, do you know where you would go?" I felt guilty for not obeying Jesus' final command to be His witness (see Acts 1:8). I was ashamed because as a pastor, I exhorted others to "share the Good News." Why is it I have no trouble telling others, even strangers, the good news about the delicious fried chicken at the Chanticleer Pub or the Illini's awesome overtime football victory? Why do I struggle sharing God's Good News? I experienced fresh freedom when I was introduced to relational evangelism and was encouraged to nurture real relationships before I ever uttered an evangelistic word.

For starters, my husband and I began to pray for our neighbors as we daily walked the cul-de-sac where we had lived for over a dozen years. We already knew most of our neighbors by name, thanks to our children's newspaper delivery job and lawn mowing service. One day I found myself somewhat unconsciously skipping over certain neighbors' names as we walked and prayed. When I pondered this omission, I saw something really ugly in my soul. I saw that I was systematically categorizing my neighbors into different groups labeled "savable," "unsavable," "maybe savable." If you were like my agnostic University of Illinois professor neighbor, you were unsavable—too smart and scientific for salvation. If you were a redneck, gun-toting, noisy partier like another neighbor, you likewise were unsavable due to the messiness of sin in your life. Then there was the divorcee, the Turkish businessman and the mixed couples of a black man and white woman, Jewish husband and Protestant wife—all "maybes" with a host of hindrances. And so it went until I realized that the only folks on my unwritten, but nevertheless very real list, were white, middle class families with nice kids like ours and somewhat "open" to church. How repulsive.

Mercifully, the Holy Spirit opened my eyes and heart. He clearly admonished me, *Take off the judge's robe*. This is a robe that cloaks our critical, judgmental attitudes with "Christian concern" for holiness. I took off the judge's robe. Through a long journey, which included an immersion into Greg Boyd's book *Repenting of Religion* and a difficult departure from Calvin's total depravity theology, I received God's forgiveness and a fresh empowerment to see all human beings as made in His image, of much worth and value. I saw each person as deeply loved by Him and pursued by Him regardless of any race, religion, redneck or rogue behavior. He is, after all, a Savior. He specializes in rescuing all. No self-cleanup required. He is full of compassion, not contempt.

> When the extraordinary compassion of God our Savior and his overpowering love suddenly appeared in person, as the brightness of a dawning day, he came to save us. Not because of any virtuous deed that we have done but only because of his extravagant mercy. He saved us, resurrecting us through the washing of rebirth. We are made completely new by the Holy Spirit, whom he splashed over us richly by Jesus, the Messiah, our Life Giver. So as a gift of his love, and since we are faultless—innocent before his face—we can now become heirs of all things, all because of an overflowing hope of eternal life.
>
> Titus 3:4–7 TPT

Let that truth seep into the soil of your heart. The seed of Jesus' love and compassion will surely take root, and fruit will be born. Our union with Jesus produces such healthy, authentic results. We can see others with His eyes and love them with His extravagant mercy and His extraordinary compassion. I hope you learn this lesson so much faster than I have.

Whether I am sitting at the Chicago O'Hare airport judging the overweight girl eating an aromatic Cinnabon or on the plane and wondering why that mother does not control her screaming toddler behind me, I still fail to truly love people as the Jesus in me loves each of them. I jump to critical conclusions. I put the judge's robe back on and judge people. Maybe the overweight girl is on her way to her mother's funeral, and food is her only solace. Maybe the wailing toddler has severe ear infections and the cabin pressure is excruciatingly painful. I do not know their stories, but I do know that Jesus loves each one, made in His image, of much worth and value.

I can choose to do the same because I am in union with Him. And He is faithful to correct me, remind me to take off the judge's robe, and help me love others as He loves each one. Sometimes, that love begins with the simple awareness of how significant each individual is.

Daily Practice

A practice that Jesus has been teaching me is to tune in to His care and appreciation for every person even when the situation is just an ordinary scene, nothing disturbing or alarming that could trigger my contempt button. For instance, I will note how thankful I am for every person who helps an airport run smoothly: the ticket agent who is sometimes grouchy, but mostly helpful; the housekeeper, older than my seventy years, who humbly cleans the bathroom toilets; the serious TSA agent, proud of his role in protecting our nation; the baggage handlers, whose strength is greater than that of a professional athlete; and the five skilled workers it takes to effectively run the busy coffee shop at eight o'clock in the morning amid lots of harried travelers. When I observe and interact with any of these ordinary people doing their job on an ordinary day at one of the world's busiest airports, filled with frustrated flyers, I realize I have a choice to smile, treat them kindly and see them as human beings, made in the image of God. I have a fresh opportunity to love others in union with Jesus. I have the chance to thank each one. Sometimes, I even have the privilege to pray for one, which would not have been possible if I had been wearing the judge's robe. Jesus loves each one and delights in letting us partake of that love and then give it away.

Try this today: Invite Jesus, who lives in you, to help you see and love people as He does. See past their skin color, clothes, weight, gender, job, ethnicity, economic status or education level and let the love of Jesus well up in you. Let the Holy Spirit reveal how unique He has made each person and how important each one is to Him and how essential each is for the flow of life here. Love each one as Jesus loves you. Paul wrote:

> Don't owe anything to anyone, except your outstanding debt to continually love one another, for the one who learns to love has fulfilled every requirement of the law . . . and every other commandment can be summed up in these words: "Love and value others the same way you love and value yourself."
>
> Romans 13:8–9 TPT

Esteem a fellow human with equal value to yourself. Value yourself as God values you. This is easier said than done. We can choose to believe what Jesus says. "So you never need to worry, for you are more valuable to God than anything else in this world" (Luke 12:7 TPT).

Jesus and I remind you to love yourself. Say this to yourself: *I am more valuable to God than anything else in this world.* It may feel awkward and selfish, but if you receive this truth and marinate in it, you are empowered to give it away. You can turn and bestow that same value on your friends and enemies alike. It takes practice and intention, but the Holy Spirit rebukes us (gently) and renews our thinking. He gives us a fresh start, again. I am grateful for that.

Sometimes, my response to others is more automatic, more a part of the transformed me. This both humbles and encourages me. I experienced this at Culver's custard eatery. My husband and I had finished our delicious meal of pork tenderloin, fries and a turtle sundae when someone said, "Hi, Happy and Di!"

We turned to see who greeted us and saw Sam, a former member of our church. We quickly learned, however, that Sam had transitioned to Samantha and now had long hair, a shapely figure and lovely clothing. I was quite surprised. What do I think about those who are transgender? I have lots of thoughts, and questions, too. I do know God created each one male or female, and that is our God-given identity. I will tell you, though, I was encouraged to feel incredible love, compassion and genuine interest in Sam's story. Sam had moved and could no longer attend our church but had found a good church home in a new city. We chatted for a few more minutes and then hugged good-bye. I did not *pretend* to love Sam—I truly experienced the love of Jesus in me flowing freely. I loved that, and I think Jesus did, too.

Jesus Has Much to Teach Us

Jesus has so much to teach us about walking in love. Whether it was a hated tax collector, a despised woman of the streets or an ostracized cripple, Jesus embraced each with compassion and care. Not so with the religious guys. They fumed with contempt at such outcasts and doubly so when they caught Jesus in the act of healing one on the Sabbath or enjoying a party in one's home. This was their response as Jesus ate dinner at a notorious cheater's home:

> Later when Jesus was eating supper at Matthew's house with his close followers, a lot of disreputable characters came and joined them. When the Pharisees saw him keeping this kind of company, they had a fit, and lit into Jesus' followers. "What kind of example is this from your Teacher, acting cozy with crooks and riffraff?"
>
> Jesus, overhearing, shot back, "Who needs a doctor: the healthy or the sick? Go figure out what this Scripture means: 'I'm after mercy, not religion.' I'm here to invite outsiders, not coddle insiders."

Matthew 9:11–13 MSG

Go figure out what this Scripture means. These are easy-to-read texts, but they require the scalpel of the Spirit in order to be lived out in our own lives. What does the Spirit need to cut away in your life? Everyone is different, so I will not be prescriptive. I will, however, repeat what Dr. Jesus prescribes: *Who needs a doctor, the healthy or the sick? I'm after mercy, not religion.* Until we feel safe to see our own sickness, our own ruthless religion, receive His merciful surgery and know He is the Healer, we are hindered from extending that same mercy and healing to others. We can be either too rigid with religion or too twisted with tolerance. Help us, Holy Spirit! Help us live this out in the 21st century, when tolerance is touted, but is ironically absent if I do not agree with the liberal lifestyle of my critic.

There are always surprises as you listen to the Holy Spirit's revelations and learn to love others as He loves. This can happen while you read or study the Bible. As I prepared to preach one weekend on the text about the lame man at the pool of Bethesda, I saw something I had not seen before. The Spirit is a great Teacher who opens our eyes. Suddenly, the word *invalid* stuck out: "Now there is in Jerusalem by the Sheep Gate a pool, in Aramaic called Bethesda, which has five roofed colonnades. In these lay a multitude of invalids—blind, lame and paralyzed. One man was there who had been an invalid for thirty-eight years" (John 5:2–5).

Obviously, *invalid* in this context is a noun, with the emphasis on the first syllable, and it refers to all the sick people around the pool. As I read it, however, *invalid* became an adjective, an actual description of those blind and lame persons. My eyes read it as "in-*valid*," with the accent on the second half. When read in that manner, the meaning of "in-valid" was clear. Someone who was in-valid was someone who had no value to society, self or others. Such people were in-valid, worthless. I saw that was exactly how these people felt and how society treated them. They had no value. They were worthless cripples. They were in-valid human beings.

But Jesus saw them differently. Jesus saw these people as valuable human beings, ravaged by the effects of sickness and sin. He demonstrated His love by healing one paralyzed man who had suffered for 38 years. Then Jesus gave him the bold injunction: "See, you are well! Sin no more, that nothing worse may happen to you" (John 5:14). Jesus had given him a brand-new identity, through and through. He was made well and could now choose to embrace the worth and value that was there all along, but had been obscured by his condition. I knew again that I wanted to see every person as valid. I wanted to be able, in union with Jesus, to remove any sickness or sin that obscures one's value.

Christ in All

I understand seeing every person as a human being, made in the image of God. I have experienced the choice I make to love each one, show compassion and care and refuse contempt. I was not, however, prepared for the next step Jesus had for me. I was not ready to see Christ in each of these persons. To see each as valuable was one thing. To see Christ in each was a totally different challenge. To say my treatment of each was equal to my treatment of Jesus? This disrupted and disturbed my beliefs and bordered on possible heresy. This was a big stretch for my conservative theology, and I had red flags of "pantheism" and "universalism" flapping before my spiritual eyes.

Many of the people I encounter daily, in my "humble" opinion (not judgment), are diseased trees full of bad apples (see Matthew 7:17). I know that many men and women I meet are not Christ followers or, like the cashier at Walmart, may even practice another faith altogether, albeit with kindness. What did Jesus mean when He asked me, *Why do you treat Me with contempt, Dianne?*

I recalled my struggle years ago when I first read a similar idea in a book about Mother Teresa, the Catholic nun who so compassionately ministered to the poorest of the poor by "seeing Jesus in each one." *How can she see Jesus in each one? How can Christ be in a sinner?*

I revisited my struggle when I read the following description by Brandon Vogt about what set her apart in an excerpt from his book *Saints and Social Justice: A Guide to Changing the World*:

> She not only served people in need, but dignified them. . . . Each weeknight her mother invited poor people into their home for dinner. . . . It was through serving these visitors that she first discovered "Jesus in his most distressing disguise." People often asked her why she loved the poor so much. . . . In response, she liked to grasp their hand, slowly wiggle one finger at a time, and

explain: "You-did-it-to-me." In her mind, you could count the whole Gospel on just five fingers. She was alluding to Matthew 25 where Jesus teaches about the final judgment. . . . "For I was hungry and you gave me food, I was thirsty and you gave me drink, a stranger and you welcomed me, naked and you clothed me, ill and you cared for me, in prison and you visited me. . . . Whatever you did for one of these least brothers of mine, you did for me." For Mother Teresa, this passage was not just a pious metaphor. It described reality. The secret to her infectious joy and boundless compassion was that in every person—every paralytic, every leper, every invalid, and every orphan—she recognized Jesus. . . . She knew, deep in her bones, that by serving others she was serving Jesus.[2]

What gripped me was the statement that she helped people because she knew deep in her bones that she was serving Jesus. And this, she surmised, was because of what Jesus Himself taught in Matthew 25. This is a challenging text—difficult to live apart from our union with Christ. I wondered, *Is there just this one text that seems to say we are serving, helping Jesus Himself when we interact with others?* Is it true that our compassion or contempt for another human is synonymous with our compassion and contempt for Jesus?

Care for Children, Care for Christ

Then, I woke early one morning and heard the Spirit say, *Read Luke 9.* Curious, I read this familiar text of Jesus and His disciples:

The disciples began to argue and became preoccupied over who would be the greatest one among them. Fully aware of their innermost thoughts, Jesus called a little child to his side and said to them, "If you tenderly care for this little child on my behalf, you are tenderly caring for me. And if you care for me, you are honoring my Father who sent me. For the one who is least important in your eyes is actually the most important one of all."

Luke 9:46–48 TPT

There it was again: *"If you tenderly care for this little child on My behalf, you are tenderly caring for Me."* Soon after I read this text and meditated on the truth about Jesus and children, I was at a training in Texas. I decided to have lunch with a good friend, Rebecca. I wanted to catch up with her and see how her daughter Abigail was doing. Abigail is a precious middle schooler who has special needs. Since I was a special education teacher for six years, I was interested in Abby's progress both as a friend and former teacher. Becca told me that things had been in chaos. The classroom teacher retired in mid-October and the district could not find a qualified replacement. Becca was not aware how chaotic it was until one day, in early November, Abigail missed her bus and Becca had to take her to school. When she walked into the classroom, she could feel the instability. She said, "I just felt totally turned off by the intense need and stress in the room. My immediate thought was I would take Abigail out of this school—tomorrow."

But God had other plans. Later, Becca spent time praying for each of her three kids. She thanked God for the precious people in their church who loved her children. She thought how when people took care of her kids, it felt equivalent to those people taking care of her, their mom. As soon as she verbalized that, she heard God say, *That's exactly how I feel*, and immediately He showed her the faces of Abigail's classmates.

Becca said, "I knew then that rather than taking Abigail out of school and escaping the need, that Jesus was inviting me to take care of Him—by taking care of His kids in this class. The next day, the district offered me the job, even though I'm only a regular, not special education, teacher. I know God heard the unspoken cries of those kids. He answered their prayers by inviting me to be there, loving Him as I loved each of them."

I was blown away. Jesus had just reinforced the truth that when we love the least, we love Him. The one who is least important in our eyes is the most important of all. Look around you today. Who is least important? The pimply teen who messes up your order again at McDonald's? The tantrum-throwing two-year-old in front of you at Target? The girl with a handicap who bags your groceries at Meijer? The child with special needs at your son's school? The homeless beggar on the corner? Can you see Christ in each one? Can you care for them? I still wrestle with this and do not claim to fully comprehend it. I want to see Christ in all.

"Put your heart and soul into every activity you do, as though you are doing it for the Lord himself and not merely for others" (Colossians 3:23 TPT). That is a good place to start. When interacting with another, picture Christ in that person. Put your heart into it. Allow the Holy Spirit to give you eyes to see. Even if you cannot reconcile this theologically (wondering if the person is saved), practice seeing and serving Christ in others. I am transformed through this practice. It has changed how I minister to people, pray for people, react to people, and finally, it has changed how I love people.

A Mystic's Encounter

I am still unsettled about all the implications of seeing and serving Christ in others, but I have enjoyed reading others' experiences of seeing Christ in all. I have been deeply impacted by Catholic saints and mystics. In her autobiography, *A Rocking-Horse Catholic*, twentieth-century English mystic Caryll Houselander described how an ordinary journey in a crowded London subway transformed into a vision that changed her life.

> All sorts of people jostled together, sitting and strap-hanging—workers of every description going home at the end of the day. Quite suddenly I saw with my mind, but as vividly as a wonderful picture, Christ in them all. But I saw more than that; not only was Christ in every one of them, living in them, dying in them, rejoicing in them, sorrowing in them . . . I came out into the street and walked for a long time in the crowds. It was the same here, on every side, in every passerby, everywhere—Christ . . . I saw, too, the reverence that everyone must have for a sinner; instead of condoning his sin, which is in reality his utmost sorrow, one must comfort Christ who is suffering in him. . . . Realization of our oneness in Christ is the only cure for human loneliness. For me, too, it is the only ultimate meaning of life, the only thing that gives meaning and purpose to every life. After a few days the "vision" faded. People looked the same again, there was no longer the same shock of insight for me each time I was face-to-face with another human being. Christ was hidden again; indeed, through the years to come I would have to seek for Him, and usually I would find Him in others—and still more in myself—only through a deliberate and blind act of faith.[3]

Yes, I, too, have seen the need for a deliberate and blind act of faith when it comes to finding Him in others and even in myself. When I sit with this mystic's account, I have a fresh resolve to treat strangers as saints (see Romans 12:13). I want to see Christ in all. I want to embrace them with fondness as friends. My experience is not the same as Caryll Houselander's, and yours is different, too. The Spirit continues to invite me into new encounters with the love of Jesus. He is ready to do the same for you. Lay aside your fears and your failures. Resolve to treat strangers as saints and picture Christ in each one.

Jesus has trusted us with an ongoing adventure—the impossible job to love people and share the Good News. I have had the privilege of traveling to many places. I have served bowls of hot rice to hundreds of Tanzanian schoolchildren, observed thousands of worn-out travelers at London's Heathrow Airport and been jostled by crazed Christmas crowds in Bethlehem and masses of people scurrying on the streets of Shanghai. I was overwhelmed. I wanted to feel compassion, but I felt contempt creeping in. It is good to know Jesus has been there, done that, and He is ready to do it again—in us.

> Jesus went throughout all the cities and villages, teaching in their synagogues and proclaiming the gospel of the kingdom and healing every disease and every affliction. When he saw the crowds, he had compassion for them, because they were harassed and helpless, like sheep without a shepherd. Then he said to his disciples, "The harvest is plentiful, but the laborers are few; *therefore* pray earnestly to the Lord of the harvest to send out laborers into his harvest."
>
> Matthew 9:35–38, emphasis added

Jesus saw the crowds. Jesus had compassion on them. The harvest is ready. It is both ripe and rotten. Harassed and helpless.

Can we see Christ in all? If so, we can count on Christ's compassion to fill us and His healing care to flow from us. We can love others in union with Jesus. My prayer is this: "Lord of this messy, helpless harvest, send me to labor in Your harvest. Flood me with Your compassion. Help me see and love You in each one."

Why Does This Matter?

A godly friend of mine, a well-known and respected man of faith, had a near-death experience and went to heaven.[4] He watched as person after person came face-to-face with Jesus and was warmly embraced by Him. Then Jesus asked all of them just one question. Only one. He did not ask how many souls they saved, bodies they healed, poor they fed or hours they prayed—as important as those things are. He did not ask how much money they gave, the number of miracles they performed or the time they spent in Bible study. Good things for sure, but what was the most important thing to Jesus as people prepared to enter into heaven's Kingdom? Face-to-face with each one, made in His image, Jesus asked this one simple question of each one: *Did you learn to love?* That is sobering to me. Have I learned to love in my brief lifetime here? I am still learning. But I want to be able to answer that question with joy and confidence. I want to know that I have learned to love in union with Jesus.

What Can I Do Right Now?

Take off the judge's robe. Stop judging others. Ask the Holy Spirit to fill you with His love. Make the decision to see every person as made in God's image, of much worth and value, re-gardless of each one's appearance or actions. Move on to seeing Christ in each one and treating the Christ in each with His love.

Father, give me eyes to see every person as one made in Your image, one of much worth and value. Fill my heart with Your love and compassion for each one.

— 8 —

Messy Ministry

*Jesus makes a mess wherever He ministers
and invites us to say yes to the "mess"
and the miracles, too.*

I REALLY DON'T LIKE MESSES, BUT I DO WANT
MIRACLES.

*Would you rather have a mess and a miracle or perfection and
pain?* the voice whispered.

A mess and a miracle . . . or perfection and pain? What kind
of choice is that? It was Jesus' voice rising up in me right along
with an explosion of anger in my chest—anger at the muddy
mess all around me.

Big streaks of wet black dirt enmeshed with sticky mounds of
freshly cut grass clippings and tiny bits of gravel and sticks—all
made a huge mess—scattered over my just polished tile floor.
Moments before, this floor shone with Mr. Clean perfection.
Now a pile of smelly socks, inside-out sweatshirts and mud-
covered tennis shoes completed the scene of mass (or should I
say "mess") destruction.

My mouth opened to rebuke my four sons and their three fellow mess makers when I stopped to listen.

Miracles are messy.

In an instant, I knew what Jesus meant. He gave me a flash-back to fifteen years prior when I longed for little muddy feet to patter across my perfect pristine floor. I was in the middle of a devastating crisis of infertility. Sure, my floor was clean, but my heart was crushed. Perfect floor. Pain-filled heart. There would be no "mommy" messes for me, the doctor had confirmed. Due to a multitude of physical problems, I would never give birth to my own child.

"Adoption is your only choice," the infertility expert had pronounced with contrition. "Apart from a miracle, you cannot conceive." To his shock, our miracle son from God arrived—seven years into our childless marriage—followed by four more miracles who filled our once-clean home with plenty of messes.

Miracle mess makers. I will take a miracle any day. I will say yes to the "mess" these miracles bring.

My union with Jesus is not just a wonderful way of life for me personally. We are sent as Jesus was sent. We are sent to set the captives free, open blind eyes and proclaim the Good News to the poor. Jesus promises us that He will work right along with us. That is good because I know I am no miracle worker. But the One in me, the God with whom I am one, said we will do the same and even greater things.

Ministry Is Messy

"Truly, truly, I say to you, whoever believes in me will also do the works that I do; and greater works than these will he do, because I am going to the Father."

John 14:12

When I first learned this startling commission that Jesus gives us, His disciples, I was super excited to partner with Jesus in performing miracles. This was so much better than the boring Christian life of just studying the Bible and attending church. Now we could do what Jesus did. We got to "do the stuff," as my Vineyard Movement mentor John Wimber said so famously in his description of miracle ministry. And there were many hurting people who were in desperate need of a ministry miracle.

What I was not prepared for, but learned quickly, was that miracle ministry is messy, because miracles do not always happen and people are not always happy. This reality can be confusing and heartbreaking for both those who pray and those who need the miracle. Ministry is messy because there are no formulas to follow, no special phrases to say, no surefire techniques to ensure miracles.

More often than not, there are messy people—they reek of alcohol, nicotine and pungent body odors. There are messy relationships—violent marriages, addicted teens and not-so-well-blended families. There are messy diseases—unstoppable cancer, debilitating Parkinson's, stubborn diabetes and mysterious Lyme disease. There are messy mental afflictions—chronic depression, panic attacks, early-onset Alzheimer's . . . and the list goes on. I know people who live with all of these conditions. I have prayed with them. Wept with them. Waited with them—for Jesus' miraculous healings.

Miracles are messy. How easily we miss this important truth when we zoom through the gospels and watch Jesus perform His many miracles in one short chapter. Ministry appears to be quick, efficient, effective, just like our reading of the text. We fail to immerse ourselves in the actual ministry moments of Jesus. There are demonized men thrashing and shrieking, contagious lepers invading an unsuspecting crowd, determined folks tearing off a roof to lower a paralyzed friend, a blind beggar screaming nonstop, a hunchbacked woman harassed by Sabbath "police" and a known prostitute crashing a religious dinner party—to name just a few of the people who received miracles from Jesus and "made" a mess in the process. Everywhere Jesus went He made a miraculous mess. Dinners with sinners. Picnics with the poor. Signs and wonders on the Sabbath. Messy mercy. If we are going to live in union with Jesus, we must gear up for the mess.

Ministry is messy in at least five different ways.

1. Ministry Messes Up Our Plans

I had just settled in for a nice quiet evening at home and the first season of *Downton Abbey*. Then came the call from a friend. Her husband had collapsed while shoveling snow and was on his way to the ER in an ambulance. Could I meet them there to pray? I rise up and say yes. But my heart sinks low as I bundle up to brave the cold and embrace the mess of ministry. Plans disrupted again.

A quick "Help me, Lord" escapes my lips, and as I drive the fifteen minutes to the hospital, He fills my heart with His compassion and replaces my selfishness with His love. He does not chide me for my reluctance. He understands the weariness of ministry and is ready to strengthen me. By the time I walk into that brightly lit, foreboding emergency room, I am filled with the compassion of Jesus. I am ready to embrace my friend and join in prayer for the full recovery of her husband. A real miracle has occurred in my heart as I said yes to the mess. And Jesus worked a miracle through our hands as we prayed for Jack and saw him made well.

Ministry messes up our *plans*, but God brings miracles out of these messes. Ministry messes up our *own lives*—our schedules, routines and our perfectly good plans. And ministry, in union with Jesus, messes with our carefully crafted to-do lists.

Keep listening as you go about your day, moving from the computer to the car to cleaning or cooking. I remind myself to listen because I can just zoom along, oblivious to our union. Jesus has things to teach us as we tune in to Him.

One day I was ruminating over the things on my schedule with some dread. I had agreed to teach a class in a nearby town, but I wanted to just chill. I tried to dismiss my dread when I heard Jesus say, *Hey, Di, I'm looking forward to going to Clinton tonight.*

Jesus wants to go? He is in me. My life is not my own. I decided I would join Jesus in His desire and drop my dread. We did have a good time teaching together. When it was ministry time, a disheveled middle-aged woman shyly came forward. Then, a tall younger man wearing greasy overalls came, followed by an elderly lady with permed gray hair who struggled to walk. I was struck by the "messy" variety in God's family. I wanted to feel His love for each, but none came. I decided to step out in faith and trust Him. I watched the presence of the Spirit overwhelm and even knock over two of these unlikely people.

It was a glorious mess. Tears flowed, unknown languages were spoken and they were all visibly touched by God. The love of God cascaded through me and washed over these precious people.

"I love how You love, Lord," I whispered. "Thank You for letting me know how much You wanted to go tonight and to give away miracles, small and large, to these precious people."

While these are impactful learning times, I am a slow learner. I default to comfort and not to Christ in me. Don't despair if you struggle. Jesus will continue to invite you to learn to love with Him. He usually does not care about our frivolous feelings or exaggerated excuses. Try not to let these get in the way of saying yes. He does not coerce us to do ministry in union with Him, but I am thankful He keeps asking. After a busy day of travel and work, I had a "deserved" desire to sit in front of the fire with a good book and avoid an event on my calendar. I was just settling in when Jesus gently said, *I'm really anticipating Holy Spirit Night tonight.*

Holy Spirit Night was the planned event, a large group gathering of worship and ministry I had decided to skip in favor of my couch and my fire. But Jesus wanted to touch people with His fire. He was inviting me to join Him in ministry. My fire or His? He gave me the choice. Like much ministry in my life, I semi dreaded it because it meant leaving my comfort zone and entering the mess. "Help, Lord!" I uttered weakly and rose to get ready.

Did I feel like it? No.

Did I want to go? No.

But I knew He wanted to, and so I said yes to the mess. I was humbled and honored to minister in union with Jesus that night as His fire of love and healing touched hundreds of hungry people. Why do I ever hesitate? I guess because I am human, and I need God in me to patiently prod me off my couch and out of my comfort zone.

2. Ministry Messes with Our Motives

I *wanted* to overflow with love for others, and I knew that I did not. This is not an instantaneous endeavor. At one time, I hoped my daily praying in agreement with this prayer would be enough to fill me with love for others: "And may the Lord increase your love until it overflows toward one another and for all people, just as our love overflows toward you" (1 Thessalonians 3:12 TPT). God answers these prayers. But often there is work to be done.

Marriage is a good analogy. We have to make changes in our behavior, our habits and our lifestyle as we grow as a couple to become one and enjoy the love that God gives. Our oneness is already a reality. The marriage certificate is on the wall and the ring is on the finger. But it takes learning and growing to experience our union of love fully.

What needs to change in my personality in order to receive the incredible love Jesus has for others, a love that lays down one's life? What needs to be wrecked in me in order to truly love others? It blows me away that I could die a martyr's death, but if I have no love, I am nothing. I could give tons of money to the poor, but if I have no love, it counts for nothing.[1] I could work the most amazing mountain-moving miracles and yet, if done without love, it means zero. Sobering. Hard to truly comprehend in our celebrity culture that is fueled by the media monster. Apart from Jesus, I not only can do nothing, but also, I am nothing. In regard to ministry, we need to be careful not to gauge how we feel, because we may feel nothing, no love at all. But we can still choose to say yes to the mess.

It always amazes me how quickly I can lose sight of the Kingdom paradigm of miracle ministry, which must be saturated with love above all else. When I get ready to minister to others, I labor over speaking the right words, being filled with mountain-moving faith, sacrificing in profound and visible ways, and yet, all of that means nothing if it is not motivated by and soaked in love. Paul reminds us,

> If I were to speak with eloquence in earth's many languages, and in the heavenly tongues of angels, yet I didn't express myself

with love, my words would be reduced to the hollow sound of nothing more than a clanging cymbal. And if I were to have the gift of prophecy with a profound understanding of God's hidden secrets, and if I possessed unending supernatural knowledge, and if I had the greatest gift of faith that could move mountains, but have never learned to love, then I am nothing. And if I were to be so generous as to give away everything I owned to feed the poor, and to offer my body to be burned as a martyr, without the pure motive of love, I would gain nothing of value.

1 Corinthians 13:1–5 TPT

This familiar love passage goes on to define in clear language what this love is like. It is God's unfailing love, not human sentiment. The only way we can experience this for ourselves and for others is when He fills us with such love. Jesus is more than happy to do this. After all, God is love. He loves to answer our heart's cry as we recognize our inability to love apart from Him.

"We can now experience the endless love of God cascading into our hearts through the Holy Spirit who lives in us" (Romans 5:5 TPT). Jesus takes His time, however, in filling us with His love for others. He makes room, rearranges and illuminates aspects of our individual personalities so we can be one with Him in love for others.

3. Ministry Messes with Our Mindsets

"We laughed, ate blueberry muffins, shared stories and exchanged some gifts, too. Everyone really enjoyed themselves. It was a blast!" Mike said excitedly. Was he recounting a recent birthday party or men's Christmas coffee group? No, this was just the usual Sunday morning gathering at the local homeless shelter where Mike and six others spent several hours sharing food, fun, fellowship and faith with grateful men and women who had no home.

A messy place? Yes.

Messy people? Yes.

Mess up your Sunday worship? Yes.

But Mike—a retired policeman—his wife, Cathy—a school secretary—and four other ordinary people show up every other Sunday to do life with the homeless who wander in each week. None of Mike's team have seminary degrees or are ordained ministers. They are simply disciples of Jesus, doing ministry in union with Him.

Everybody, not just trained, degreed ministers, gets to play or pray. It is as simple as showing up and loving others. Sometimes, if someone shares a need, you may ask a simple question: "Can I pray for you right now?" These are just seven words anyone can ask—anywhere, anytime. This is not just for full-time church employees. This is for all of us. Whether we are acquainted with a person or not, we almost never have someone reject this offer of prayer.

Most people are surprised that we mean we will pray right at that moment, not later when we get home. Many have never had anyone offer to pray for them in person, even those who are regular church attenders. Most welcome this out-of-the-ordinary, yet simple, tender touch. It is natural and, at the same time, supernatural. We like to say it is "naturally supernatural" and not at all "repulsively religious." The great thing about this simple offer of prayer is that we can do this almost anywhere—in the Costco checkout line when the clerk says she has a bad headache or in the bleachers when the mom next to us is concerned about her injured daughter or at the office when our workmate is distraught about his upcoming review.

Each person has a unique sphere of influence. It takes some trial and error to discover your best ways to partner with God. Burnsey has many great conversations on her train rides to Chicago. Heather notes who needs encouragement at the spa. Toni prays for those who come to the food pantry. Charles stays alert in his apartment building for those in need. We do not have to know a special script or carry our Bible. On the contrary, we carry Christ in us, and His love flows out of us.

We are in union with Him, and He shows us what He is doing in our day, along the way, to help the people He loves through us. Jesus ministered so powerfully because the Father is always working. He told His disciples: "Truly, truly, I say to you, the Son can do nothing of his own accord, but only what he sees the Father doing. For whatever the Father does, that the Son does likewise. For the Father loves the Son and shows him all that he himself is doing" (John 5:19–20).

It seems crazy (yet encouraging) that Jesus could do nothing on His own. Jesus did only what the Father showed Him to do, and He was very aware that He could only do that. The Father loved to show Jesus what He was up to. Jesus just had to be alert and obedient. It is the same for us. Some might say, "Yes, but Jesus had an advantage—He was, after all, the Son of God. He had special intimacy with the Father."[2] Jesus has given us this same advantage—we are all sons and daughters of the Father, in intimate union with God.

4. Ministry Messes with Our Pride and Platform

"Miracles in Mozambique!" This headline shouted from the glossy cover of the Christian publication. I quickly turned to the page that recounted multiple instances of raising the dead, feeding and housing hundreds of destitute orphans and many other wonderful healing miracles on the continent of Africa. While my heart leapt at the recounting of Heidi Baker's miraculous ministry, I could feel the familiar jab of jealousy poke me in the chest. "When am I ever really going to do the greater works of Jesus like Heidi?" I uttered with some despair, some disdain. Despair because I did the ungodly "compare" with another, and disdain because I did the sinful disgust with myself. Miracle ministry messes with our pride and our platform, both of which are nauseating realities in the 21st century, probably more than ever before.

Despair and disdain are often lurking nearby to rob us of the joy we experience when we say yes to the mess of miracle ministry. We live in a social media milieu that constantly screams about everyone else's marvelous ministry and miracles. There are Facebook videos to watch, testimonies to read and the ever-present encouragement to "share," "like," buy the book, invite for a conference and send in a donation to participate in the amazing work the minister (I mean, God) is doing somewhere in the world. My cynicism is only because I am well acquainted with this ugliness in myself.

Amid all the urgent imperatives to "discover your destiny" and "embrace your divine purpose" there runs a real pressure to promote yourself, build a platform, garner the fame (I mean, fruit) that shows you are God's man or woman of the hour and you walk in obedience to His call on your life. This promotion is often pride, poorly disguised as pleas and prayer requests for the people my miracle ministry is touching. This is especially a problem in the world of messy miracles where you are often only as good as your last miracle and are easily replaced by the latest miracle worker. How opposite the ministry of

Jesus that we have been given to do in union with Him. Paul wrote,

> Be free from pride-filled opinions, for they will only harm your cherished unity. Don't allow self-promotion to hide in your hearts, but in authentic humility put others first and view others as more important than yourselves. Abandon every display of selfishness. Possess a greater concern for what matters to others instead of your own interests. And consider the example that Jesus, the Anointed One, has set before us. Let his mindset become your motivation.
>
> Philippians 2:3–5 TPT

I am wrecked all over again when I read those words and allow them to penetrate my whole being. Who can honestly live this way? No one. That is the point. We must be wrecked for God and live in the union He so graciously invites us into. Only then can we do the same and greater works. Only then can we partner in the true messiness of miracles with the only One who can do miracles. When we humbly embrace our humanity, our ordinariness and our equality with one another in the family of God, we enjoy a freedom from comparison, competition and pressure, and we can enjoy ministry in union with Jesus no matter how messy things are. Does this mean I never post on Facebook or have a website or share a story? Of course not. It does mean we need the Holy Spirit to monitor our motives, responses and methods.

5. Ministry Messes with Our Ego

The mission of our church is a bold statement: "Change the world with Jesus!" This has many positive aspects to it.

Everybody wants to make a difference. We do not do it alone, but with Jesus. I have discovered, again, as an Enneagram Three, this mission constantly sets me up for the f-word—*failure*. Failure, the feared fallout of ministry gone awry. Failure, which is unacceptable to me, but not to God. I do hope to change the world by ministering healing to those who are suffering. That is Jesus' ministry, and that is mine as His disciple.

I obediently prayed for my friend Barb to be healed of a mysterious pain that would not relent. She was touched by God's love, but in spite of my pleas, she was not touched by His healing. She died at the young age of 56 years. In my mind, I have failed. I set out to change the world once more and counsel a young couple with a troubled marriage. I am hopeful. God brought them together. I performed their simple wedding in the park and surely, this marriage can be saved. They have three children who need a two-parent home. Sadly, that home was destroyed by divorce. I have failed again. Infertile couples who never conceived, graduates who failed their boards, entrepreneurs who filed for bankruptcy and a child who refused to reconcile—so many ministry failures in my attempts to change the world with Jesus. Ministry in union with Jesus is not a guarantee of one hundred percent success and zero percent failure. Far from it. But we can have one hundred percent freedom from fear of failure.

What if nothing happens when we pray or minister? This is a real fear. It fools us into thinking it is up to us to make sure a person is miraculously touched. We are not responsible for the results—God is. Apart from Him we can do nothing. He is fine with handling the results, even when we think "nothing happened." The least that happened is the person experienced God's love. I was taught an important truth by John Wimber, founder of the Vineyard Movement: "It's okay to fail." We do not flunk if we fail. John himself learned this the hard way; he prayed for more than two hundred people over the course of many months before seeing anyone healed.[3]

Will we fail? Yes, in the sense that we do not always see actual healing or change. Will we make mistakes? Lots of them. It keeps us humble, dependent on Jesus and aware: God does the work in all of us. The Father is better than any earthly father, and He is not bothered by our failure. He is delighted that we took a risk, stepped out in love to pray or care for someone, then trusted Him for the results. By the way, the Father Himself does not call any of this "failure." He calls it faith. Faith that pleases Him.

Changing the world is a big task even if I try to do it with Jesus. One morning, in that early dark before dawn, I was half awake thinking about the burden of "changing the world with Jesus" that day. I thought maybe I would just take a vacation from this vocation when I heard that gentle whisper of the Spirit. *Don't change the world with Jesus today.*

What?

Instead, He continued, *love the world today with Jesus.*

Yes, that is not quite so measurable. Love can be difficult, but I will trust the Holy Spirit in me to fill me with overflowing love to love the world today in union with Jesus. If I use the word *change*, I feel too much pressure. But when something good does happen and change does occur, I take too much praise.

Pressure and praise. I will let Him change others because that is the business He is in. And maybe He is not even asking me to love "the world," but for today, I can just "love the one"—the slow-moving one in front of me at Sam's, the one fussy grandchild sitting at my table, the one driver cutting me off in traffic, the one I have been married to for almost fifty years and can take for granted. Yes, today I will just "love the one with Jesus."

Replacing the words *change the one* with *love the one* gives me a different attitude toward people. I no longer approach them with the thought that they need to be changed. Such an attitude really stinks, and believe me, people can smell it. They can smell that I think I am better than they are and I am there to fix them. Defenses go up and hearts shut down. Maybe I never think those things, but I communicate my "fix-it" attitude when I go about my day looking for someone to "change." How much better to let the Spirit fill us with the compassion of Jesus, then watch and feel the difference His love makes. His mercy never fails.

Mercy Is Messy

As we walked into the building, I could not help but notice the inappropriate clothing on a number of people who walked beside us. We were surrounded by pony-tailed men and spiky-haired women wearing short shorts, tank tops, sloppy sweat-pants, flip-flops and even no shoes at all. The ample exposed skin was covered with the smoky ink of multiple tattoos and piercings in outrageous places. I swallowed hard and looked away, feeling—oddly—both superior and insecure in my A-line skirt and modest blouse. "Well, we are in Southern California," I mused, "and the weather is really hot." But this was not a sporting event. This was a church service. Then, out of the corner of my eye I noticed several questionable guys snuff out cigarettes before entering the foyer. Had we come to the wrong address? The warehouse did look more like a club than a church, and clearly these folks looked like they were more ready to party than to pray. But this was a true church—a collection of sick in need of a doctor (see Matthew 9:12), a plentiful but help-less and harassed harvest ready to receive the mercy and heal-ing that Jesus was eager to release (see verses 36–37). We had gathered at a church, but it was a church as Jesus intended—a hospital for sinners and not a museum for saints.

Jesus said, "I desire mercy, and not sacrifice" (verse 13). What a painful lesson to grasp.

Time for me to be wrecked for God, to abandon self-generated sainthood, self-efforts to heal people and sinful pre-requisites I put on others. It was time for me to receive an explo-sion of Jesus' mercy in my own heart—a must for all miracle ministry. Messy mercy. Many messy tears flowed that night as I encountered the compassion and mercy of Jesus—His mercy for messy people, including messy me. This messy mercy and crazy compassion of Jesus changed everything when it came to ministry. I was wrecked for God and for good as I encountered a whole new paradigm for ministry. This paradigm for ministry did not tell the sick that in order to be healed they must "meet God's conditions" or "get more faith" or "clean up" their messy lives. No, this paradigm lavished mercy, compassion and the unfailing love of God on all. Healing comes with compassion. Miracles follow mercy.

> On one occasion, a leper came and threw himself down in front of Jesus, pleading for his healing, saying, "You have the power to heal me right now if only you really want to!" Being deeply moved with tender compassion, Jesus reached out and touched the skin of the leper and told him, "Of course I want you to be healed—so now, be cleansed!" Instantly his leprous sores completely disappeared and his skin became smooth!
>
> Mark 1:40–42 TPT

Deeply moved with tender compassion. The fact that God
is full of compassion has been disputed in the past. Ken Blue,
author of *Authority to Heal*, says:

> Among the elements in traditional theology which have deterred
> us from praying effectively for the sick is the all-too-common
> notion that God is emotionally removed from our suffering.
> . . . "Most theologians rejected feeling as a divine attribute. For
> them it connoted 'weakness.'" . . . The Bible teaches that God
> was in Christ, and therefore he not only cares deeply about
> our pain but also has experienced it. . . . In the New Testa-
> ment, we find a Greek word for compassion (*splanchnizomai*)
> that gives exquisite testimony to God's caring for our pain
> and to His determination to alleviate it. . . . The word used
> to describe His compassion expresses the involuntary gasp
> wrenched from a man overwhelmed by a great sorrow or the
> groan of a woman savaged by labor pains. Out of this deep
> compassion sprang Jesus' mighty works of rescue, healing and
> deliverance.[4]

When I first read these words written by Ken Blue years ago,
I knew I wanted to be a woman of Christlike compassion. I
wanted to feel true compassion for the hurting. I knew the
powerful pains of labor. I knew the fierce feelings of mother-
hood. I wanted Jesus to fill my heart with such an all-consuming
compassion for the sick and suffering. He did, and He has done
that over and over, but it is never a "done deal." Our union is
dynamic and growing, not static and stale. But I can forget
that simple truth, take it for granted and fail to be moved with
compassion.

I sat down in my favorite chair with my computer and a fresh
cup of steaming coffee. I was ready to work on this chapter. It

was a beautiful, but cold, February morning and I had a full three hours of uninterrupted time. Perfect writing conditions. Too cold to be tempted to be outdoors but brilliant sun to encourage creativity. I sat and sat. I struggled. Words would not come. I checked my phone. I sipped and stared. Why could I not write about a subject I loved—mercy and compassion in ministry?

Then came the familiar voice of the good Shepherd. *Today I want you to walk in compassion, not write about it.*

Was He talking about the memorial service I was going to skip? After all, it was for an older woman who had been part of our church years ago but had moved to another state. I had thought about stopping by, but it seemed so disruptive and unnecessary, especially now that I had determined to spend this morning writing. Her children probably were not too devastated, and I barely knew them. But I guess Jesus wanted to go and touch the grieving family with His compassion.

As I was preparing to go, Jesus prompted me to grab a package of new sheets I had just purchased. They did not fit the bed and would need to be returned for a refund. *Why not just drop them at the Goodwill instead of returning them to Home Goods? It's right by the funeral home,* Jesus said. *Someone would love new sheets instead of the nubby, worn ones!*

Compassion and comfort for a Goodwill shopper—and for a grieving family. Sounds like Jesus.

At the memorial, I enjoyed reconnecting with my friend's son (who was indeed grieving). Then, when viewing all the family photos, I was overwhelmed with the compassion of Jesus. I surveyed the memorabilia of a life lived in loving union with her Lord. Tears filled my eyes when I saw her favorite devotional on the table: *My Utmost for His Highest* by Oswald Chambers. A fitting description of her life and a reminder to me of what is truly important. As I headed home, I noted I still had a good hour left to write. But Jesus had other ideas.

Why not drop in and see Rick? said the voice in my mind.

No, I don't think that is Jesus speaking. I need to get home and work.

Except, I found myself turning in to the rehab center where 69-year-old Rick now lives despite his frequent objections. Born with cerebral palsy, Rick lived independently for years. He attended church by wheeling his chair on the sidewalk over two miles. He worshiped and prayed with enthusiasm even though he has never spoken an actual word. Now, he can no longer care for himself and must receive help with daily tasks. That is so hard for this fierce fighter who still trusts God for healing and longs to live on his own. He told me (through painfully pointing to his letterboard with his crippled hand) that his mother is dying. *Just like your mom*, he adds. I am touched that he remembers. Compassion and love filled our brief thirty-minute conversation, and we even had the opportunity to pray with his aide, a beautiful woman from Liberia. As I left, I thanked Jesus for every wonderful worker at this less-than-perfect "home." They are compassion in action.

Who can you care for today with the compassion of Christ? What nudges from the Holy Spirit can you respond to? Of course, most are not convenient. They come at random moments, and we have just a moment to respond. I have missed so many of these. I always seem to have good reasons why I cannot do as I sense I am to do. But Jesus in me is patient and persistent. He genuinely designed us to partner with Him in ministry, despite our messy misses. Often, these opportunities are ordinary, everyday things happening all around us.

So how do we partner in ministry with Jesus? Where, when and how does our union with Him make a difference as we obey His command to "heal the sick, raise the dead, cleanse lepers, cast out demons" (Matthew 10:8)?

With this type of ministry, we learn quickly that apart from Him we can do nothing. This is both the best news and the worst news. We are, after all, "mere men." This is what Paul so poignantly remarked after miraculously healing a lifelong cripple and subsequently being "worshiped."

"Friends, why are you doing this? We are merely human beings— just like you! We have come to bring you the Good News that you should turn from these worthless things and turn to the living God, who made heaven and earth, the sea, and everything in them."

Acts 14:15 NLT

Yes, we are merely human beings—women and men filled with God—yet mortals for sure. It can be dangerous to think otherwise. It is God, not us, who made heaven and earth and who alone has the power to heal crippled feet that have never taken a step. And in the most incomprehensible sort of way, we are in union with this miracle-working God. He lives inside each of us and sends us to continue His ministry with the guarantee He never leaves us and works with us. Let's learn to trust Him with the miraculous results.

Why Does This Matter?

Joining Jesus in His messy ministry is the real reason we are here. That does not mean we drop everything and enroll in Bible school or seminary to get trained for the ministry. Some might, but the great thing for many of us is that we get to do this in the course of our regular rhythm of life, messes and all. It does not matter if we are a banker, butcher or bus driver. This is a miracle ministry and that guarantees we cannot do this without Jesus, the miracle worker. Good thing He lives inside us. Good thing He loves to partner with us to bring healing and hope to those around us. Good thing He is patient and persistent in our doing ministry together. I am getting used to His messy ministry. I am getting better at being alert and available to His desires (with the occasional selfish slip). And I delight when miracles happen. But the real miracle in all of this is the total transformation in each of our messy lives as we do ministry in union with Jesus. We are God's messy miracles.

What Can I Do Right Now?

Start to partner with Jesus in ministering to others. Listen for His voice today and cooperate with His will. Be okay with the messes. Offer simple prayer, encouragement and love to those who come across your path. Expect the compassion of Jesus to flood your soul. Leave the results up to Jesus. He can handle His reputation, so don't worry about Him or you. Come on— get messy!

Holy Spirit, help me see those You are touching today and empower me to partner with Your compassion and healing.

— 9 —

Powerful, Not Pagan

Jesus knows best how to pray in power.
No more pagan prayers, please.

MY PRAYERS SEEM WEAK IN SPITE OF GOD'S PROMISES.

Screams filled my ear as I held the phone and tried to hear
my daughter. Her one-month-old infant could not be con-
soled, and now my daughter was convinced that the baby's
recent surgery had gone terribly wrong. "Why did I agree
to this, Mom? What if she can never really communicate? I
made a big mistake. I'm a terrible mother," she said, sobbing
uncontrollably.

After a few tense moments, I managed to get the full picture that had created so much fear and fury. Usually, I would
run across the street and try to assist in person, but I was two
thousand miles away, sitting in a sun-soaked chair, gazing at
the Pacific Ocean. Jerked out of my rest, I tried to stay calm
as I gave some practical advice and promised to pray until I

heard back. I had no sooner clicked good-bye when fear crept in like an unwelcome fog. It blurred my ability to see reality and caused me once again to bump into a familiar wall—a wall of petrified prayer, stonelike and programmed—a formidable wall of pagan prayer.

Like a pagan, I was tempted to start begging God for help, repeating mindless, faithless pleas for healing. Pagans are those who usually have a religious practice that is marked by ritual, repetition and bargaining with a higher power. I had been here before when trouble struck and powerless prayers stuck in my throat. Jesus warned about such prayer:

> "The world is full of so-called prayer warriors who are prayer-ignorant. They're full of formulas and programs and advice, peddling techniques for getting what you want from God. Don't fall for that nonsense. This is your Father you are dealing with, and he knows better than you what you need. With a God like this loving you, you can pray very simply."
>
> Matthew 6:7 MSG

This is a stern but helpful rebuke from Jesus. He makes it clear that not all prayer is productive. In fact, it is downright pagan. Pagan prayer is repetitive, formulaic and transactional. Such prayer is filled with techniques for getting what we want from God. This kind of prayer is tempting and seems to promise much. I should know. I have read many books on prayer that prescribe faith formulas. I have tried the outlined steps. I have followed the formula: Pray. Wait. Repeat. I have hit this wall before. I am thankful for the Holy Spirit's help in cultivating a life of prayer in me for the past forty years. And I am thankful He is still working in the sometimes hard and weedy soil of my life, especially when trouble strikes and prayer problems protrude again.

Instead of praying for my sick granddaughter as a pagan would, I prayed in the Spirit, lying on my beach chair in the warm California sun as the Pacific Ocean roared in my ears, reminding me of the greatness of the God with whom I spoke. I prayed softly, persistently with words I did not know but I trusted He knew and heard. I fixed my mind on my precious granddaughter and imagined her being enveloped with the healing presence of Jesus, two thousand miles away. And I waited.

Forty-five minutes later, my daughter called to say things were calmer but not really better. I chose to trust God's goodness and asked Him—now with my own words of English—to continue His work of healing, wisdom and help. I thanked Him for His love and care. Twenty-four hours later, Molly and Mama had turned a corner with helpful medical advice and the wonderful healing touch of Jesus.

Thank You, Holy Spirit.

Holy Spirit, Help!

When faced with the heart-wrenching crisis with my youngest grandchild, I once more found how my first response could easily be formulaic prayer. I was tempted to fight or take flight, but neither formula is Jesus' way to pray in union with Him. I know I do not "fight the devil." Jesus already did that. Such crazy shenanigans we often try in the name of fervent prayer. These resemble pagan pleas. I do not fight, and neither should I take flight (i.e., flee to my religious reserve of rote prayers). It is tempting, though. Why are formulas so much easier (at first) than friendship? Friendship with our loving Father is much better, especially when it comes to conversations (prayer) about the things that weigh heavy on our hearts. Things like a depleted bank account, a fractured relationship or a sick grandbaby. I would rather choose friendship over formula any day, but sometimes I still struggle to remember Jesus' words and the truth they speak: *This is your Father you are dealing with, and He knows better than you what you need.*

How do I pray in union with Jesus? How do I intentionally engage with Him who lives in me and ask Him how to pray for Molly and Julie? I am not trying to get Jesus to come down and fix the problem. He is here. He is in my daughter. He is in me. He is here to stay. He is listening. He is ready to help. I can pray in union with Him, confident of His love and power, too. There is no formula for prayer. There is friendship with our loving, all-knowing, all-powerful God, who is our Father. This is not a transaction between two people. Prayer is a conversation of trust between a loving God and a needy child. Jesus reminds us of what the Father wants for us:

> "Do you know of any parent who would give his hungry child, who asked for food, a plate of rocks instead? Or when asked for a piece of fish, what parent would offer his child a snake instead? If you, imperfect as you are, know how to lovingly take care of your children and give them what's best, how much more ready is your heavenly Father to give wonderful gifts to those who ask him?"
>
> Matthew 7:9–11 TPT

The Father wants to give wonderful gifts to those who ask Him. Contrary to what some religious "experts" teach, our good God is not giving my grandbaby irreparable surgery damage. Why do we say and believe such things? When our prayers go unanswered or we are confused about the goodness of our God and His unfailing love for us, we default to such terrible theology. That is twisted and results in a hard heart and destroys trust in our loving Father. The Father wants good things for His children. He does not give rocks instead of bread or snakes instead of fish. He does not give cancer instead of a cure or heartache instead of healing. He gives wonderful gifts to those who ask, but He wants us to ask, and to ask persistently.

> "Ask, and the gift is yours. Seek, and you'll discover. Knock, and the door will be opened for you. For every persistent one will get what he asks for. Every persistent seeker will discover what he longs for. And everyone who knocks persistently will one day find an open door."
>
> Matthew 7:7–8 TPT

Ah, persistence! That does muddy the water—and the words—of prayer. Herein is the temptation to beg, plead and hence, once again, pray like a pagan. How can I pray with persistence? My prayers seemed to hit a wall. My granddaughter continued to struggle and my daughter was desperate. I needed to persist in prayer. *Help, Holy Spirit!* That is it, precisely. The Spirit is so happy to help. He is the Helper after all. He lives in us, making our union with God alive, real and active. One of His favorite activities is to help us with prayer.

> The Holy Spirit takes hold of us in our human frailty to empower us in our weakness. For example, at times we don't even

know how to pray, or know the best things to ask for. But the Holy Spirit rises up within us to super-intercede on our behalf, pleading to God with emotional sighs too deep for words. God, the searcher of the heart, knows fully our longings, yet he also understands the desires of the Spirit, because the Holy Spirit passionately pleads before God for us, his holy ones, in perfect harmony with God's plan and our destiny.

Romans 8:26–27 TPT

The Holy Spirit does the persistent pleading on our behalf. He is "super-interceding" for us and our desperate dilemma. "Super-interceding"—that is the official Greek rendering of that verb, which describes the type of prayer the Holy Spirit is praying. He is pleading persistently and passionately. We can fully trust what He is saying because it is in perfect harmony with God's good will. But how do we do this? What are the emotional sighs too deep for words? For me, this is where the gift of a private prayer language, praying in an unknown language, is so valuable. I do not know these words. They are deep, emotional utterances from my heart as I pray in union with the Holy Spirit, trusting He knows best. And He does. It may not be obvious immediately, but He is orchestrating good in response to our prayer together. We need to be convinced of that.

"We are convinced that every detail of our lives is continually woven together to fit into God's perfect plan of bringing good into our lives, for we are his lovers who have been called to fulfill his designed purpose" (Romans 8:28 TPT). In the case of my sick granddaughter, we received what we asked for. But not all agree this is the way of prayer. Can we ask for what we want, or is that too selfish?

Pray in Union with God's Word

"Prayer is not about getting what you want," warned the teacher with a serious tone. "Prayer is about God getting you where He wants. Stop treating God like a cosmic butler."

This sounds spiritual, but it is one of many half-truths that are pounded in the pulpit and end up hurting our pursuit of a healthy prayer life in union with Jesus. True, prayer is much more than a transaction of getting what I want. That is an apt description of pagan prayer. But prayer is not just an exercise of wrestling with God until He gets me where He wants me. What kind of relationship is that? I know prayer is not getting what I want when I want in a manipulative way. There are many mixed-up prayer practices, even in Christian prayer. People need encouragement to pray about all things. Prayer is not a transaction, but it is also more than just a time to talk with Jesus or a time for God to transform me. Prayer is a time to ask. Jesus wants us to know this: "If you live in life-union with me and if my words live powerfully within you—then you can ask whatever you desire and it will be done" (John 15:7 TPT).

How do I pray in union with Jesus on a daily basis? To pray in Jesus' name is to pray in union with Him. This has several implications, but all center around praying according to Jesus' will. In the past, this had caused me angst because first, I was clueless about His will and second, I was sure when and if I discovered it, it would not be remotely close to my will.

Surrender, surrender, surrender, insisted the voice of religion. Those echoes in my ear implied that the will of Almighty God was something difficult and in a place so remote it would take a long trek through the jungle to arrive. There is a surrender of my will, but a good, confident surrender.

This is a surrender, not to an enemy whose will and intentions for us are harmful and horrible. No, this is surrender to One whose will is wonderful, joyful and the absolute best for each of us. The Word of Faith movement, while fraught with its own set of difficulties, did positively open my eyes to the truth that I can know God's will. I do not have to live in constant confusion. I can be assured that God is a good God who wants good things for me. This was the most powerful truth I discovered in the middle of a difficult and heartbreaking season of infertility. All the other voices in my life—the doctors, pastors, family and friends—said confidently, "It must not be God's will for you to have children, because obviously you can't get pregnant." Then I learned that God's Word said the opposite. And I discovered this in a King James Bible, no less, so it must be really true. (Smile.)

"He maketh the barren woman to keep house, and to be a joyful mother of children. Praise ye the LORD" (Psalm 113:9 KJV).

Suddenly, I knew my long-sought-after answer to what is God's will. In addition to this single promise, there was a host of other stories of barren women whom God blessed with babies—Sarah, Rebecca, Rachel, Hannah, Ruth and Elizabeth. God's Word could be trusted to reveal His will. I could ask in Jesus' name—in union with God's will—and know He heard me, was pleased and wanted to answer. This changed my life as I defied all medical prognoses and religious rationale and gave birth to not one but five children. God answers prayer according to His will, and we can know His will from His Word. I am cautiously aware of how misused this truth can be. People find isolated texts. They play Bible roulette, letting the Bible fall open and speak to difficult dilemmas, and they end up doing dumb things that alter their lives. They give away all their money like the rich young ruler or nail themselves to a cross to be crucified like Christ—because they were confident of God's will from His Word. It is best to invite the Holy Spirit to add His confirmation to our confidence.

God's Word and its revelation as God's will changed the way I prayed, in union and in harmony with Him. For many years I have selected portions of Scripture, mostly prayers already recorded for us by David in the book of Psalms or Paul in the epistles or Jesus in the gospels, and I have "prayer-a-phrased" these. I adjusted them for my personal prayer. I am confident I am praying God's will because I am praying His Word. I am praying in union with Him. One of my longtime favorite prayers is this, which I have paraphrased from Colossians 1:9–12 NLT:

> We ask you, God, to give us complete knowledge of your will and to give us spiritual wisdom and understanding. Then the way we live will always honor and please you, Lord, and our lives will produce every kind of good fruit. All the while, we will grow as we learn to know God better and better. We also pray that you will be strengthened with all his glorious power so you will have all the endurance and patience you need. May you be filled with joy, always thanking the Father. He has enabled you to share in the inheritance that belongs to his people, who live in the light.

When I use Scripture, sometimes I do just "say my prayers." I fall into rote repetition without much feeling, faith or awareness of my union with Jesus. But as I am consistent and persistent, I find that God so graciously answers. Praying God's Word is such an easy resource for praying in union with Him.

Choose a few prayers that are meaningful to you right now. If you want, change the pronouns (like I did above with the Colossians prayer). They are not just the prayers of Paul, but your prayers. Begin to pray these in union with Jesus. Note how faith rises in your heart. Peace floods your mind. You are praying God's will, in His name. He hears and answers you.

What Do We Talk About?

Communication. Most marriage therapists, books and pastors list communication as one of the top essentials for a healthy, enduring marriage. In a similar way, our "marriage"—our union with Jesus—is kept healthy, vibrant and growing through communication. Our love deepens as we talk with one another in prayer. Our communication with Jesus may be casual, peppered with, "Thank You so much, Jesus," or "I love You, Lord" or "I really need some help, Jesus!" These are meaningful and precious to us. Ray Moran, in his book *Spent Matches*, says:

> This journey (of learning to walk with God) is one person growing to know and trust another. It requires constant exchange of meaning to allow the relationship to grow. Our Western minds want to compartmentalize that exchange of meaning into a box called prayer. It is unfortunate that we cordon off our communication with God into this box. In a Hebrew way of thinking, people relate to their Father in a moment-by-moment basis, not in a compartmentalized box. As we move along in our journey, we hear from God, we ask, plead, cry out, share, complain, and thank. . . . We are never out of ear shot of His ever-present care for us, yet we often feel far from Him. The nature of our deepening relationship with God is found in

giving regular attention to Him and accepting His ever-present attention to us.[1]

Giving attention to Him is not hard because He lives right inside us and He never leaves. This has often been referred to as "practicing the presence" of Jesus.[2] I like to think of such conversation as more than the practice of the presence of Jesus where I parrot phrases to Him (as I have done in the past). I like to view it as participation in His presence, in me. Participation is more intimate than mere practice. This is something every one of us can begin today as we go about our daily routines of work, exercise, chores, caring for others, driving, grooming, etc. When you pray, you are not only recalling, practicing the fact of Jesus' presence in you; rather, you are engaging with Him as though He were sitting right next to you as you drive to work or standing with you as you chop vegetables for the salad or running with you as you prepare for your marathon. You are in conversation with the One who loves you, lives in you and never leaves you.

As in any relationship, it can be difficult to know what to talk about every day. Prayer is no different. People are often stymied by what to pray on a daily basis. We seem to run out of things to say. My prayer life was radically changed when I learned the simple way of praying the way that Jesus taught. We can be one hundred percent sure we are praying in union with Jesus when we pray the Lord's Prayer. When asked by His disciples to teach them to pray, Jesus replied with a simple, powerful prayer that covers all the bases of daily life and can be done whether you are sitting on a plane, kneeling by your bed or cheering on the sidelines.

Our Father in heaven, may your name be kept holy. May your Kingdom come soon. May your will be done on earth, as it is in heaven. Give us today the food we need, and forgive us our sins, as we have forgiven those who sin against us. And don't let us yield to temptation, but rescue us from the evil one.

Matthew 6:9–13 NLT

There are lots of resources on how to effectively pray this, but I like the simple way of using the different sections of the Lord's Prayer as a prompt and then talking with Him about each topic as it relates to the things going on in my life that day. I listen for His voice, the voice of the good Shepherd, as I pray.

For example, I pray, "Please bring Your Kingdom, Your will, this day to my mom so her pain is lessened and she can eat." Jesus speaks gently to me, and the suggestion pops into my mind to take her a favorite soup from Panera Bread that is easy for her cancer-ravaged throat to swallow. I plan to do that next time I visit.

Jesus and I continue talking with one another as I use the words He gave me to pray. "Jesus, today I really need Your daily food of wisdom, empowering me to write. I appear to be blocked." I wait and listen. I am reminded of a podcast that encouraged me to find my voice, and I decide to relisten in response to this prompting from Jesus.

Our conversation continues. "Forgive me for losing my cool with the sales clerk yesterday. I want to always reflect Your love to others." I then received fresh assurance of Jesus' forgiveness and His empowering to love in union with Him.

I finish with, "Jesus, please deliver my friends from evil today as they travel to the Ivory Coast." I wait until peaceful images replace the haunting ones in my mind.

This time of prayer may last one minute or one hour, depending on the needs and concerns in my life and the lives of my family and friends. The Lord's Prayer gives us a skeleton on which to hang our current needs with the assurance that we are praying God's will in union with Jesus. The result is a healthy prayer life. No longer do we need to strain, strive, moan or groan. Jesus is in me. Jesus is in you. He loves to join our prayers and give rest to our worries and fears as we talk—pray— together as one. His Kingdom come and His will be done. But . . . His will is not always done, because for now, we are in a battle. There are Kingdom collisions all around us. How do we pray when collisions come?

Kingdom Collisions and Prayerful Persistence

The call came late at night. I heard it by the third ring and grabbed the phone, my heart already involuntarily pounding. Is there any more frightening sound that pierces our peaceful sleep than the ring of our phone? We instinctively know something is wrong. It is somewhat unusual to receive a call after 10:00 p.m., but it was especially concerning when I saw it was from our youngest son, Cory, who lives in Chicago. He usually has to get up between four and five o'clock in the morning, so he goes to bed early.

"Don't worry," said my daughter-in-law, Jenna, calmly. "But Cory is in an ambulance on his way to the ER. His heart is doing funny things." Not worry? She explained that he had been having unusual chest pains for over an hour and had finally decided it was something serious enough to call 911. This is a guy who is super healthy, eats right and trusts God's healing power with strong faith. I knew it was serious if he agreed to an ambulance. My stomach knotted immediately.

What do most people do when a crisis hits? I am thankful we do not have to cajole God into answering or plead with Him to pity us and intervene. He is here. He is in us. We are in union with Him. Whenever the call comes or the crisis hits, I usually respond with fear first, faith second and worship last. I wish that were not true, but it is. Jesus wants to enable us to jump for joy when we encounter "the grief of many trials" (1 Peter 1:6 TPT) and to praise Him in the pain. He is truly the good Shepherd who walks with us (and in us) "through the valley of the shadow of death" (Psalm 23:4). We need fear no evil. But we do. The battles are real. We live in the clash and tension of two kingdoms—the Kingdom of God and the kingdom of darkness. Paul wrote,

> Your hand-to-hand combat is not with human beings, but with the highest principalities and authorities operating in rebellion under the heavenly realms. For they are a powerful class of demon-gods and evil spirits that hold this dark world in bondage.
>
> Ephesians 6:12 TPT

While Satan and his minions are defeated, they are not departed. The Kingdom of God is already here, but not yet fully consummated. There will be what I call kingdom collisions. It is good to know, though, that Jesus has all authority and shares that with us. We have this command from the same chapter: "Be supernaturally infused with strength through your life-union with the Lord Jesus. Stand victorious with the force of his explosive power flowing in and through you" (verse 10 TPT).

We can stand victorious with His explosive power flowing in and through us because we are in life-union with King Jesus. How do we battle the ferocious fear that threatens to consume us? How do we calm the crazy pictures that flood our minds? How do we quiet the storm of voices that scream in our ears?

How do you combat the fear that wants to consume your entire being when you hear the news that another kingdom collision has just occurred? How do you respond when you suddenly encounter the clash of the evil forces of the kingdom of darkness and the Kingdom of God?

I wish I could tell you that I calmly went to "I will sing in the middle of the storm." No, that would have to come a bit later. Thankfully, the Holy Spirit did well up within me with His prayer—that prayer in an unknown language—that gave me His words when I did not know how to pray in my fear and desperation. Thank God for the gift of tongues. I wanted to lie down and hope all was well. But I got out of bed and headed down to the sofa, where I now was fully awake.

First, I reminded myself that Jesus lives in me. We are in union. I pray in His name, and this is not a phrase I tag on to a prayer to perform some spiritual magic. I handed my fear to Him and asked Him for His healing, peace and Kingdom to come. I waited to sense His presence. Not easy. But He is faithful.

I have had to remember that Jesus is not only in the storm, but He is also *in me*. It does not always feel like it. Even after many years, it is not automatic to recall this truth that I have believed, taught and now write about. Storms disrupt our faith, even faith that is solid, tested and tried. Jesus has patiently taught me how to be more at rest in the storms—those times when I experience kingdom collisions of this type. I have learned to relinquish self-effort and my temptation to show Him what a big girl I am and how I can handle collisions on my own—not.

My childlike trust, rest of faith and choice to rejoice demonstrate to the evil forces all around that they must depart. I choose to trust and worship the one true God, and His name is

Jesus. Prayer, at these times, is best expressed through worship. Whether you grab your phone and listen to a favorite playlist or you grab your Bible and join with the songs of the Psalms, just do it. Worshiping and rejoicing in times of trouble have a miraculous way of calming the soul and allowing the faith of the One who lives in us—the faith of God—to rise.

Thankfully, less than an hour later, Jenna called with the medical personnel's good report that Cory was overstressed for a thirty-year-old, but his heart was healthy. There would be no overnight stay in the hospital. There had not been the attack I had feared—the mysterious heart ailment that had killed my husband's 47-year-old brother and was possibly genetic. Relief and rejoicing flooded my entire being.

While this prayer was answered quickly—as far as prayers go—it was still unsettling and intense. Many prayers do require more persistence. Pesky persistence is the one area we are most likely to engage in those pagan practices I mentioned earlier—begging, pleading, manipulating—in hopes of changing God's mind or cajoling Him to answer quickly. Persistence is also the main attribute of a so-called prayer warrior. I am not even sure there is such a designation, because it reeks of self-effort and work.

Paul does exhort us to put on the full armor of God, which a soldier would wear to war. He then details this armor in warrior language, concluding with the admonition to "pray passionately in the Spirit":

> Put on God's complete set of armor provided for us, so that you will be protected as you fight against the evil strategies of the accuser! . . . Because of this, you must wear all the armor that God provides so you're protected as you confront the slanderer,

for you are destined for all things and will rise victorious. . . .
Pray passionately in the Spirit, as you constantly intercede with
every form of prayer at all times.

Ephesians 6:11, 13, 18 TPT

There are many teachings about this armor of God. The
majority focus on what *we* do (we put on, we fight, we use every
piece, etc.). We expend our energy in order to protect ourselves
in times of intense spiritual battle. That is exhausting! This
armor is a beautiful picture of our union with Jesus. He is our
truth, our holiness, our faith, our peace, our salvation. As we
live in the reality of this union, the battles are fought—that is
for sure—but they are fought in union with Jesus. This is in
sharp contrast to putting on a full armor, waving an unwieldy
sword and hoisting a large shield against the enemy in our own
strength as we prance in some nebulous spiritual realm.

There is a dance in prayer—a war dance of sorts. This dance
is not begging, but believing. This dance is not wrestling, but
resting. From God's side, this is a partnership of persistence.
Persistence is not the art of convincing God. Persistence is
needed because we are up against the resistance of the enemy,
not the resistance of God. Together, in union with Jesus, we
turn and mount a resistance to the enemy with persistence.

"Surrender to God. Stand up to the devil and resist him and
he will turn and run away from you" (James 4:7 TPT).

Resistance is real. There are cosmic forces unleashed against
us and they must be resisted in union with Christ. Jesus does
exhort and instruct us about persistence in prayer in two different texts (see Luke 11:5–8; 18:1–8) where a reluctant friend and
an unjust judge refuse to answer the request, but persistence
prevails. In these texts, God is not the reluctant friend or the

unjust judge. This is contrary to what many have been taught. This can result in pagan prayer—begging, pleading, trying to figure out how to convince this reluctant, resistant, even unjust God to answer prayer. The resistance is from the enemy, who is similar to the evil, unjust judge. The enemy can even assume the behavior of a rude and reluctant friend.

But Jesus teaches us that we must persist. Persist in believing that our God is good, He loves us, He hears us, He knows what is best. He is doing all He can in this mysterious cosmic climate of kingdom collision. The enemy notes our persistence and reluctantly releases his hold.

Do I understand all of this? No, but I believe it. When we maintain our persistent faith, worship and communication with our Father while we wait for our answer to prayer, we demonstrate we believe He is the one true God, and all other gods must flee. Then, the answer comes. There are no formulas for this. This is the faith of the One who likewise wrestled in prayer. I often forget this. I know Jesus was a man of prayer, as documented by the gospels. But I overlook His most difficult time of prayer in His life, and I put it in the exception category. That was my mindset until I endured a tough night in my own "Garden of Gethsemane." I am in no way comparing my situation to Jesus' time of prayer. I did not sweat blood, but I learned some important lessons on how to pray in union with the One who did.

Can You Pray for One Hour?

The text read: *Emergency surgery at midnight. Could be two hours. Very serious. Please pray.*

I omitted some of the personal details of this text, but this was a life-threatening situation for a young mother of three children. How do you pray when your mind immediately fills with dialogue from the devil? How do you turn off the terrible images of a widowed, devastated husband and three mother- less children? How do you pray when every fiber in your being is gripped with fear? I am so thankful for the gift of praying in the Spirit—of praying in tongues. So that is where I started. I prayed in the Spirit. I kept my mind set on my union with Jesus. While the accuser whispered condemnation for my weakness and fear, the Spirit reminded me that Jesus, the One who con- quered death, had joined our intercession and was continually praying for triumph over tragedy.

> Who then is left to condemn us? Certainly not Jesus, the Anointed One! For he gave his life for us, and even more than that, he has conquered death and is now risen, exalted, and enthroned by God at his right hand. So how could he possibly condemn us since he is continually praying for our triumph?
>
> Romans 8:34 TPT

Not only does the Holy Spirit pray for us, but so does Jesus Christ. Two divine intercessors pray for us each day. Two-thirds of the Trinity are actively engaged in intercession for us. Peace came as I meditated on this. I was not begging God or trying to convince God; I was intense, focused and joined by God Him- self. When Satan the liar tried to tell me Jesus was serendipitous and unreliable, I was thankful the Spirit could bring to my mind the many Scriptures that reminded me plainly who Jesus is, how He healed the sick, what He taught on prayer, His promises of hearing and answering. Faith comes by hearing the Word.[3]

After one hour of this war in union with Jesus, there is still no word. I am tired. It is late. Then, I hear the Lord's challenge, *Could you not tarry one hour?* He quoted the King James version of His night in the Garden of Gethsemane when His three closest friends were not able to stay awake while He prayed earnestly to the Father on the eve of His crucifixion: Yes, "the spirit indeed is willing, but the flesh is weak" (Matthew 26:41 KJV).[4] I knew I had to continue praying for another hour.

Almost exactly one hour later, I heard a text come. I fumbled to grab my phone and read it with my heart pounding. Tears burst forth as I absorbed the news that surgery had been successful. As I reflected the next morning on the whole experience, I began to beat myself up for fighting so much fear and anxiety, all the while knowing Jesus is in union with me. Why could I not trust Him more? Why did I fail to have faith? I sensed I was to read the account of Jesus in the Garden since this was what came to me in the night. I saw that Jesus, in His humanity like us, pleaded earnestly with the Father, falling on His face in deep distress.

I saw that He, too, fought fear, anxiety and oppressive sorrow as He asked three times, "My Father, if it be possible, let this cup pass from me; nevertheless, not as I will, but as you will" (Matthew 26:39). The devil's resistance was real. Jesus' persistence was needed. A cosmic battle was in full progress. An angel came to strengthen Him. I know this passage is often taught as a model for relinquishing our desires, but I think that cheapens its more profound meaning. Brian Simmons had this insight in his commentary from *The Passion*:

> "If possible, take away this cup of suffering." The cup becomes a metaphor of the great suffering that Jesus had to drink that night in the garden. However, Jesus was not asking the Father

for a way around the cross. Rather, he was asking God to keep him alive through this night of suffering so that he could carry the cross and take away our sins. . . . The "cup" he was asking God to let pass from him was the cup of premature death that Satan was trying to make him drink in the garden. . . . God answered his cry . . . so that he could be our sacrifice for sin on Calvary. Jesus did not waver in the garden. We have a brave Savior.[5]

I am so thankful we have a brave Savior. He lives in each of us and releases His courage and His faith in us. But the battle is real. The fear is felt. He never chided me for my "faith failure" or my anxious attitude. He gave me wisdom on how to pray in this situation. There are no formulas. Just simple faith and solid friendship. We do have to talk with Him about how faith is to be exercised in every prayer situation as we pray in union with Him. God's answers may surprise us, but we can trust Him. He is a faithful Friend and a good, good Father.

Why Does This Matter?

God wants to answer our prayers. He promises this over and over as He issues invitation after invitation in His Word to "ask." It is quite easy, however, to default to "pagan prayer"— where we beg, plead, manipulate, repeat and bargain with God, oblivious to our union with Him. Prayer becomes a rote ritual, and answers are absent. I encourage you to let the Spirit teach you how to pray in union with Jesus and not only get answers to prayer but also get to know Him better and love Him more.

--------------------- ***What Can I Do Right Now?*** ---------------------

Invite the Holy Spirit to help you and commit to one new way to pray—the Lord's Prayer, Scripture, in the Spirit—and do this every day for just ten minutes, aware of your union with Jesus.

Father, thank You for the privilege of prayer and Your patient persistence in teaching me to pray as Your precious child and not as a pagan.

Bonfire or Hellfire?

God is a consuming fire. Let Him prune those dead branches so you can produce abundant fruit.

BUT I'M AFRAID OF THE FIRE!

"Flee or fry! Turn or burn!" the zealous youth worker declared as he thrust his Bible in the air and slapped the leather for emphasis. The restless group of teens sat on the cold, hard ground and stared into the campfire whose flames were an eerie, unintended visual of the choice their leader presented. Such "fiery" evangelism has been a mainstay in Christian circles since long before Jonathan Edwards preached his most famous sermon, "Sinners in the Hands of an Angry God," where he pictured God holding sinners over the fires of hell and then warned his congregants to "turn or burn." Fear of hell has provoked no small number of people to turn to God in order to escape an eternity of torment.

Hell is a hot topic—literally and figuratively. In the 21st century, there has been an explosion of books and blogs debating the topic of hell. This is not a chapter on hell, despite the title. I will not dissect all of those beliefs but will assert my belief in a final judgment and the importance of one's faith in Jesus. I do know that I want to spend eternity in union with God, enjoying all the marvelous things He has prepared for those who love Him. I am looking forward to a heavenly, eternal home filled with the presence of God and the presence of saints from every tribe and tongue.

My motivation for loving God is not compelled by a desire to escape the flames of hell. I know Jesus has taken my judgment at the cross and my eternal destination is settled. That has been a liberating truth for me. I got regular warnings that hell awaits the disobedient and "you never really know" until the judgment day where you will spend eternity. While that warning instilled in me a fear of the devil's fire, I suffered more from a fear of God's fire and a misunderstanding of His burning passion for me. I did not know how His love for me was at times a consuming fire in the present and not a judgment to be feared in the future. This is not a chapter on how to be ready for the judgment of God, but on how to cooperate with the "burning" of God in our lives now.

Fire is a common metaphor in the Scripture for God's sometimes unpleasant but, nevertheless, always helpful work that brings true transformation. We need not worry or be fearful. It is safe for each of us to be wrecked by and for God. He truly walks through the fire with us (see Isaiah 43:2) and in us. This has been a tough lesson for me to learn and live. I discovered that I had to constantly remain aware of the success of Jesus' finished work, the indwelling power of the Spirit, my indissoluble union with God and the unfailing love of the Father for me while I was in the fire. I continue to "learn and burn." Yet, I am thankful that the One who "baptizes with fire" is the One who lives in me and you.

On May 6, 2018, I was on my knees in my home office, where forty-one years before, to the date, I'd received my first baptism of the Holy Spirit. There was such a sweet, strong sense of God's presence. I was thankful and weepy with gratitude for my husband, our children, our grandchildren, our church and God's faithfulness. I was struck again how revolutionary that baptism in the Holy Spirit was for my whole life. As I worshiped, He spoke these words: *I'm giving you a new baptism, a baptism of fire.* I was familiar with the phrase and concept "baptism of fire." This was sometimes preached and prayed for as the fire of God coming into our lives—an impartation from the Spirit of fresh energy and an increased empowerment to pray for the sick and move in the spiritual gifts. I knew I needed that, and it was quite exciting.

He continued, *This is not what you think. This baptism of fire is My consuming fire, to bring true transformation in all of your life.* I had struggled with some despair over the bad fruit of anger, impatience and jealousy in my life and had recently journaled about it. I recalled the first place in the Scripture where this term, *baptized with fire*, is mentioned and turned to read it again (a good habit when the Spirit speaks words that are already spoken in the written Word).

John the Baptist announced,

"I baptize you with water for repentance, but he who is coming after me is mightier than I, whose sandals I am not worthy to carry. He will baptize you with the Holy Spirit and fire. His winnowing fork is in his hand, and he will clear his threshing floor and gather his wheat into the barn, but the chaff he will burn with unquenchable fire."

Matthew 3:11–12

As John proclaimed the arrival of Jesus, most of his hearers would have thought these words signified the arrival of the final day, the final judgment and the establishment of the Kingdom of God on earth. Most were aware of a prophesied coming of the Spirit and the One who would judge with fire any unfruitful and unrepentant person in the last day. But Jesus brought God's Kingdom in an unexpected way—God's rule over sin, sickness, Satan and death—right now through His person, ministry and, ultimately, His death and resurrection. God's rule, His Kingdom, is already here and yet not fully here, until the final day. "God did not send His Son to the world that he may judge the world" (John 3:17 YLT) but to bring eternal life to all who believe. People can respond with repentance and receive a new life immersed in the Holy Spirit and fire, as witnessed on Pentecost.

As I read this text, I saw afresh that it is easy to read harsh judgment into such texts, and there is some legitimacy with that, but we need the full context. Even the reference to burning the chaff can have multiple meanings. That is what the Spirit pointed out to me. He told me I have chaff in my life. I have unfruitful branches. He went on, *Dianne, this is a fire—a baptism of fire—to burn all chaff or all branches that are not producing fruit in your life. This is for further transformation as we live in union with one another.* It was the Spirit's personal invitation to a present bonfire, not a future hellfire.

Hence the invitation to you to a bonfire—your own personal campfire with God, where He frees you from any dry, dead or

216

distracting wood, hay or stubble. This is His fire to consume the chaff that hinders you from living in the reality of who Jesus has already declared you to be.

I have discovered that despite the sometimes painful and uncomfortable process of being pruned, and consumed, I emerge being more fruitful than ever. All the while I remain confident of my union with Jesus and assured of His unfailing and unconditional love for me. There is such a paradox in pruning and the ensuing burn of the branches.

A Lesson on His Fire

On a recent spring night, a bonfire roared in my backyard amid mounds of branches, even some with spring greenery, waiting to be thrown onto the flaming stack of sticks in the fire pit. This is my husband's favorite time of year. He spends hours balanced precariously atop a ladder that is leaned against the thick branches of our tall Bradford pear tree as he, somewhat systematically, saws away. He then maneuvers his dangerous trimmer gingerly among the slender euonymus bushes, whose rapid growth threatens to shade our swimming pool. From tree to tree, bush to bush, this is springtime pruning in full gear.

As I gazed at my backyard, I had a brief time of mourning. The pear, sweet gum and plum trees looked stunted and deformed, a far cry from even their bare wintertime beauty. The spindly, trimmed-back bush branches resembled crooked, bony fingers reaching into the empty air. Our beloved roses stood stark and ugly, cut to the core, amid the gray soil of the garden. And yet I knew, from years of experience, that my backyard would soon be our own beautiful, lush Garden of Eden. The trees would flourish with shades of green, the bushes would burst forth with layers of leaves, and the roses would once again unfold their fragrant buds of red, yellow and pink flowers.

The paradox of pruning is one of Jesus' most important lessons for those who wish to enjoy the fruit He has for us.

> "I am the true vine, and my Father is the vinedresser. Every branch in me that does not bear fruit he takes away, and every branch that does bear fruit he prunes, that it may bear more fruit. . . . If anyone does not abide in me he is thrown away like a branch and withers; and the branches are gathered, thrown into the fire, and burned."
>
> John 15:1–2, 6

I am aware that some teach these texts as "turn or burn" texts. They say that those of us who bear fruit will be pruned by the Father for increased fruitfulness. I agree with that. On the other hand, they go on to say that those who do not bear fruit are taken away and those who refuse to abide in Jesus are thrown away and burned in the fire, just like my backyard branches. Either a person is completely in or a person is completely out of the fire. When this text is compared to others in the whole Bible, however, I can see these dead, unfruitful branches differently. I see them not as complete persons who are in or out, but rather, these dead, unfruitful branches are seen as specific things in our lives that need to go—to be pruned and burned.

These might be habits that hinder our growth like watching too much TV or drinking too much wine. Or these could be the nasty gossip I still delight in or the unforgiveness I refuse to release. I am not "burned in hell" for these. My union with Jesus is dampened by these behaviors, and His image in me is somewhat obscured by this willful sin. After all, I am not bearing the Spirit's fruit of love or self-control. But Jesus still lives in me and me in Him. That is settled by His work on the cross.

As I have reread John 15, I have been struck by the words "He takes away" (verse 2), meaning they are completely removed. The Spirit spoke and said, "Behold, the Lamb of God, who takes away all sin of the world!" (John 1:29). I knew He was reminding me again to live in the reality of the astounding gift of total forgiveness of sin—sin that has been taken away—by the shed blood of Jesus. Sin, not just covered up, but removed by Jesus' sacrifice, leaving us holy and complete in His sight. This is *not* automatic but must be received by faith.

"And by his one perfect sacrifice he made us perfectly holy and complete for all time! . . . And then he says, 'I will not ever again remember their sins and lawless deeds!'" (Hebrews 10:14, 17 TPT).

Was the Spirit interpreting this text to mean that the sins I was struggling with were taken away already and I should stop struggling, turn from them and receive the gift of forgiveness and empowerment to live in that reality? Had I become too sin-conscious and not Savior-conscious? I had always thought this text in John 15 meant that some branches (i.e., people) were clipped off Jesus, the Vine, because they were disobedient and unfruitful and then cast into the fires of hell. Perhaps that is what it does mean on one level. For me, however, I knew the Spirit was highlighting a greater truth, and that truth has brought transformation to me, a real cleansing through His spoken message (see John 15:3) and a reminder of the powerful gift of all my sins being forgiven and my life transformed into a new creation. While I already knew these truths, I was prompted to more carefully tune in to the "washing of water with the word" (Ephesians 5:26) in my life.

For example, when I do a daily reading of the Bible, I have often experienced certain words or phrases that "leap out" at me. I know this is the Holy Spirit highlighter. He wants me to stop and hear what He has to say. I was reading in James 3 one day when these words suddenly jumped out: "For wherever there is jealousy or selfish ambition, there will be disorder and every other kind of evil" (verse 16 TLB).

I knew this was a warning, and I received it as a washing of the Word. I had a fresh determination to stop being jealous of other women speakers and writers. This was a current struggle, and I knew it was wrong. Instead of being defensive or ignoring this Spirit revelation, I was quick to ask for His help to live as a saint and not a sinner. This type of interaction with the Spirit and the Word is one of the best ways to receive the pruning of the Father. In some aspects of my life, however, where I am more stubborn or hard of hearing, I need some fire—refiner's fire, that is. Not hellfire. This refiner's fire is not to destroy me, but in order that I can fully enjoy my union with Jesus now—and forever. I discovered we can actually welcome the refiner's fire.

Refiner's Fire

Bloggers and preachers alike have shared the following story[1] of how a silversmith refines silver in the fire, but it is worth repeating here. A woman was doing a Bible study about God as a refiner in her life and decided to discover if what she had read about the refiner's fire was true. So she visited a silversmith and watched him work.

As she watched the silversmith, he held a piece of silver over the fire and let it heat up. He explained that in refining silver, one needed to hold the silver in the middle of the fire where the flames were hottest to burn away all the impurities. The woman thought about God holding us in such a hot spot; then she thought again about the verse that says: "He will sit as a refiner and purifier of silver" (Malachi 3:3 NIV). She asked the silversmith if it was true that he had to sit there in front of the fire the whole time the silver was being refined. The man answered that yes, he not only had to sit there holding the silver, but he had to keep his eyes on the silver the entire time it was in the fire. If the silver was left a moment too long in the flames, it would be destroyed. The woman was silent for a moment. Then she asked the silversmith, "How do you know when the silver is fully refined?" He smiled at her and answered, "Oh, that's easy—when I see my image in it."

Before I truly understood my union with Jesus, I did not like this story or the truth it illustrated. I knew Jesus lived in me and His image was not something I was trying to attain via good behavior or good works. For a season, I decided the refiner's fire was not an accurate illustration of God's activity in my life. I knew Him as my Father, I argued. I knew Him as a friend and as the faithful Lover of my soul. I knew He had made me blameless in His eyes through Jesus' sinless sacrifice (see Colossians 1:22). Hence, I was wary of being ensnared again by old religious teachings.

Those were teachings that had distorted God's character into that of some sadistic monster, taunted me with the fear of never being good enough and left me twisted in fear at the Father's refining fire. Why would He throw me in the fire? That seemed wrong, very wrong. But wait. I discovered upon closer examination that He did not throw me in the fire and leave me there to be destroyed by my horrible, hot circumstances. He held me, carefully, with His eyes fixed on me and His hand steady and sure until the right time. He was not burning up the old, sinful me. That death happened at the cross with Jesus. I did not have two natures. I had the righteousness of God in Christ. I was a new creation, conformed to the image of Jesus Christ. The Spirit patiently taught me that there is no contradiction in my righteousness being real and the refiner's fire being right.

Just because I had some dross, the unwanted material that forms on the surface of molten metal, this in no way negated the truth that I am now pure, holy, righteous and clean "silver" in His sight and in my being. That dross could be outright sin, like telling a lie, unfairly judging another or constant complaining and grumbling. Those are all sins for which Jesus has already forgiven me, and yet His fire—or the flames from my own foolish behavior—alerted me to stop living in a way that denied the truth of who He has made me to be as a new creation.

On the other hand, that dross could also be the good works I continue to perform in order to gain approval from God when He has already approved of me in Christ. This latter issue is one I have struggled with because of my bondage to religion and a performance-oriented personality. As I continued to ponder the refiner's fire in my life, I studied 1 Corinthians 3:11–17. This study refocused me on the truth that any self-efforts, no matter how good and noble, if not generated from a foundational trust in Jesus and His finished work, were synonymous with wood, hay and stubble that will burn. Such works would be destroyed by fire—now or later. Why not now? Why not concentrate on building with gold, silver and precious stones (i.e., the teaching of the cross and Jesus in me now)? Why not look to the cross's glorious effects in my life, the fruit that this bears and the image of Christ in me that this truth magnifies?

Paul wrote,

> The quality of materials used by anyone building on this foundation will soon be made apparent, whether it has been built with gold, silver, and costly stones, or wood, hay, and straw. Their work will soon become evident, for the Day will make it clear, because it will be revealed by blazing fire! And the fire will test and prove the workmanship of each builder.
>
> 1 Corinthians 3:11–12 TPT

I asked the Spirit to show me the wood, hay and straw in my life—any area where I was still bound by religion, self-effort and good works. How was I relying on these to gain favor with God and man instead of having faith in Jesus' work? Where was this "fuel for fire"? The Spirit was ready to show me. Good works can be so deceptive because they feel good. It feels good to hand out food at the food bank, to give a big tip at the restaurant, to stop and help a homeless guy or to rake leaves for an invalid neighbor. There is nothing bad about all that good. But if I do these things apart from my union with and true love of God in my heart, such works are nothing and will burn. I keep doing such good things, but I do all in union with Jesus, aware of His love, energy, direction.

I want to build with that gold, my union with Jesus Christ. I want to shine like gold and have a golden faith, His faith in me, that comes through the fire—whether that fire is from God, the enemy or my own stupidity. "If his work stands the test of fire, he will be rewarded. If his work is consumed by the fire, he will suffer great loss. Yet he himself will barely escape destruction, like one being rescued out of a burning house" (1 Corinthians 3:14–15 TPT).

Everyone's work will be tested. I asked the Holy Spirit to test my work now, in the present. He was happy to help. I quickly learned I was too concerned with pleasing people and receiving their admiration under the guise of doing good things for God. How did I discover this? When my Facebook post only received a few "likes" and zero "shares" and my video only had twenty views (compared to my friend's one hundred), I was down and depressed. When I opened my email and read a scathing critique of a message I had preached from my heart, I reeled from the rejection. When my friend failed to acknowledge the kind favor I had sacrificed to "perform" for her, I was miffed.

This was my work being tested in the scrutiny of real life, and it was all fuel for the fire. I repented for wanting the praise of men. It is so flattering, but oh, so fleeting. I want to do all that I do in union with Jesus with the full knowledge that I am one hundred percent loved and approved by Him, whether others notice or not. I want to write, speak and live as a righteous daughter, thankful for God's gifts and freely giving them away as He empowers and directs me. We are one through the success of the cross.

Not all I have taught and believed has been confirmed in the heat of God's refining. Rather, some things have gone up in the smoke of God's fire. I am grateful for the flames that devoured my beliefs about the importance of my efforts, the need for me to relentlessly run after God and the pressure for me to discern God's will or miss Him entirely. I gladly watched that me-centered mess (and more) be replaced by a Christ-centered consciousness that brought true transformation and real rest.

Why wait until the final day to have a bonfire in my life? I am in union with Jesus now. I am His home now. I am made new and clean in my being. This is an ontological truth—one that freed me from sin consciousness and redirected my entire life to Savior consciousness. I am forever thankful for this freedom. I am also thankful for the fire. I am eternally grateful that I am God's home and He is keeping me clean. "Don't you realize that together you have become God's inner sanctuary and that the Spirit of God makes his permanent home in you?" (1 Corinthians 3:16 TPT).

Sadly, I have watched others who have been set free by the glorious message of grace and our righteous identity as saints who then have tried to deny that there were a few dead branches hanging on their trees or a few unwanted materials floating around in their lives. This denial thwarted the work of transformation that the Spirit wanted to do in order to make Christ's image more visible and vibrant in their lives. They incorrectly surmised that if they acknowledged some sin or bad habit in their lives, that somehow this denied the truth of the success of the cross, the new creation and their identity as righteous saints.

I do understand their hesitancy because I, too, struggled with this supposed inconsistency. If I am a saint, how can I also be a sinner? The truth is, I am a saint who is sadly choosing to sin, and that is different from having two natures. I must make the choice to cooperate with the Spirit as He shows me areas of my life that need to be pruned and burned so I will bear much fruit and reflect the accurate image of my Lord.

Meanwhile, this does not alter the reality that I am in union with Jesus and He alone is my foundation. I have wrestled with this tension of trouble and the truth of my redemption. I have fought with the fire, so to speak, but Jesus has patiently taught me and, most importantly, transformed me in and through the fire. I am confident of the Father's love for me. I know He is not an abusive father who throws me in the fire. He is a faithful

Father who holds me and molds me in the fiery trials of life here on earth. And I know Christ is in me, in the fire, and He is praying for me as the flames roar. Because Jesus knows there is another roar in our ears, and that roar can rob us of our faith.

A Faith That Does Not Fail

Jesus prays that our faith does not fail. This is important, because He knows sometimes it is the enemy who roars and who does the sifting in our lives, testing our faith. Our enemy, Satan, is a real being who seeks to devour us and destroy our faith in God.

Peter, one of Jesus' closest friends, wrote this letter to suffering saints: "Be well balanced and always alert, because your enemy, the devil, roams around incessantly, like a roaring lion looking for its prey to devour. Take a decisive stand against him and resist his every attack with strong, vigorous faith" (1 Peter 5:8–9 TPT).

Peter had firsthand experience of the devil's ruinous attempts to seek and sift. One time, Jesus alerted Peter to an upcoming assault from Satan: "Simon, Simon, Satan has asked to sift each of you like wheat. But I have pleaded in prayer for you, Simon, that your faith should not fail. So when you have repented and turned to me again, strengthen your brothers" (Luke 22:31–32 NLT).

Satan's sifting can be scary and confusing. But Jesus is on top of it. Jesus assured Peter that prayers were said for Peter. Jesus prayed for Peter's faithfulness through this difficult test of faith. Did some chaff come loose in Peter's life as he was pummeled, shaken by Satan's sifting?

Yes. Scripture reveals Peter's devastating denial of his beloved Master, not once but three times. Chaff for the fire. But we later get a glimpse of the man Peter became after he experienced

Jesus' restoration (see John 21:15–22) and the Spirit's Pentecostal empowerment (see Acts 2:1–41). Peter obeyed Jesus' instruction to share his experience so others could be strengthened when Satan sifts us like wheat.

Thank you, Peter, for writing 1 and 2 Peter. Thank you for encouraging us in the fire of our trials. "These trials will show that your faith is genuine. It is being tested as fire tests and purifies gold—though your faith is far more precious than mere gold" (1 Peter 1:7 NLT).

I know Jesus is praying for each of us when we are in the throes of Satan's sifting. This has strengthened me not only when I was sifted like wheat, but also when each of my children and other loved ones faced severe tests of faith. My confidence has been bolstered knowing that, through every trial and sifting from Satan, Jesus is praying for our faithfulness that our faith "may not fail" (Luke 22:32). I am so glad we are in the fire together and Jesus has burned up my distorted beliefs and forgiven my foolish failures. For a while, I believed (incorrectly) that since Jesus lives in me, I should not experience failure, suffering or even chastisement. But what kind of father doesn't discipline the children he loves?

The Father's Discipline

"If you move out of this house, there will be no car, no cash and no coming home for your mom's meals or laundry service. You're on your own." These were my husband's stern and anger-filled words. His face was set with a finality that was inflexible.

Our oldest son, our "miracle from God" firstborn, sneered, slammed the door and stomped out with fierce defiance. He might as well have just stomped on my heart. It was crushed.

Even worse was the worry. Would he follow through and make the move to the summer sublet apartment on the nearby college campus? In our city, this was a popular habit of many high school graduates who wanted to get a jump start on their fall freedom and partake of the party life now. Our son had been invited to join a group of four friends—footloose and fancy-free friends—whose parents were not the stick-in-the-mud duds that we were. But we knew this booze and babe hangout would be the worst place for our son. He was already struggling with his faith and was vulnerable to teenage temptation and campus craziness.

I knew all this. I knew my husband was right in his response. And yet, my mother's heart hurt. In our eighteen years of mutual parenting, we each had our roles. My husband was the tough, toe-the-line, no-excuses, "because I say so" dad. I was the tender, "let's have mercy," "tell me how you feel" mother. Tough and tender. Our children needed both in order to grow strong in character. But it was not easy to keep the balance, and there were plenty of conflicts between his coarse correction and my compassionate cries. What a picture of our heavenly Father! He is a "consuming fire" (Hebrews 12:29) and "full of compassion" (James 5:11 NIV). We need both, but we do not always delight in this discipline.

Maybe we, like those of old, have forgotten. . . .

And have you forgotten his encouraging words spoken to you as his children? He said, "My child, don't underestimate the value of the discipline and training of the Lord God, or get depressed when he has to correct you. For the Lord's training of your life is the evidence of his faithful love. And when he draws you to himself, it proves you are his delightful child." Fully embrace

God's correction as part of your training, for he is doing what any loving father does for his children. For who has ever heard of a child who never had to be corrected? We all should welcome God's discipline as the validation of authentic sonship. For if we have never once endured his correction it only proves we are strangers and not sons.

Hebrews 12:5–8 TPT

Such a powerful reminder of everyone's need of correction in this crazy world of questionable conduct and "Christian" character that is not Christlike at all. All you need is love, love, love . . . and lots of life-giving discipline from our God. We need His consuming fire to create in us His character.

God corrects us throughout our lives for our own good, giving us an invitation to share his holiness. Now all discipline seems to be more pain than pleasure at the time, yet later it will produce a transformation of character, bringing a harvest of righteousness and peace to those who yield to it.

verses 10–11 TPT

Pain and pleasure. Tough and tender. We need both in order to become the truly transformed children of our Father and healthy, contributing members of society. Father Richard Rohr addressed this necessary tension in his book *Falling Upward*:

For any of you who might think this is just old religious moralizing, I offer the wisdom of Eric Fromm, in his classic book *The Art of Loving*. He says that the healthiest people he has known, and those who very often grow up in the most natural way, are those who, between their two parents and early authority figures, experienced a combination of unconditional love along with very conditional and demanding love! . . . I know this is not the current version of what is psychologically "correct," because we all seem to think we need nothing but unconditional love. Any law, correction, rule, or limitation is another word for conditional love. It is interesting to me that very clear passages describing both God's conditional love and also God's unconditional love are found in the same Scriptures, like Deuteronomy and John's Gospel. . . . Our naive sense of entitlement and overreaction against all limits to our freedom are not serving us well as parents and marriage partners, not to speak of our needed skills as employees, students, conversationalists, team players, or citizens. It takes the pain of others to produce a humane and just civilization, it seems.[2]

I know there are many who have suffered agonizing abuse at the hands of parents and persons in authority. That is tragic. That can mess with your mind when it comes to the Father's discipline. I pray you can trust His goodness, love and wisdom when He brings positive, but perhaps painful, correction in your life. This is not punishment. I pray all of us can submit to His consuming fire of correction, knowing it will bring a harvest of righteousness in our lives. Once I stopped fearing the Father's discipline and instead welcomed it, I could discern it in so many places. I chose to receive it rather than reject it. I stopped trying to rationalize my "bad" behavior.

For example, I opened my email one day, thinking the note was a fun connection from a new friend. Instead, I read a harsh rebuke concerning my actions at a recent outing we attended. I was humiliated, embarrassed and defensive. How dare she accuse me and have the gall to write me? My blood boiled. Thank God for the cooling presence of the Spirit. As I listened to the Holy Spirit, He confirmed that I did speak unwisely at this gathering and I was wrong. An apology was needed. An adjustment in my careless speech was imperative if I wanted to grow as a leader and as a righteous daughter of my Father.

Painful? Yes.

Profitable? By all means.

Punitive? No.

We grow in the process by which the Father brings His faithful fire of loving correction.

> Since we are receiving our rights to an unshakeable kingdom we should be extremely thankful and offer God the purest worship that delights his heart as we lay down our lives in absolute surrender, filled with awe. For our God is a holy, devouring fire!
>
> Hebrews 12:28–29 TPT

A campfire, not hellfire, is waiting. So come to the Father's fire, receive His tough love and be wrecked and transformed for good. We are His children, born into a new, unshakable Kingdom, and He deserves our absolute surrender.

By the way, all five of our children survived our tough and tender discipline. And by God's amazing grace, and with lots of grit and gratitude, all of them have thrived and become healthy, godly adults. That oldest son? He is now the father of five rambunctious children and the pastor of hundreds who are learning to welcome the Father's course—I mean, coarse—correction. He well knows that such correction yields a bountiful crop of Christlike character. He calls his people to the fire and the fruitful freedom of the Father's fierce love.

Why Does This Matter?

God does not transform us overnight. He does not change us instantly or automatically. And when that happens, our impatient egos are not happy. But when we trust our union with Jesus, we can know that we are made new, holy and righteous in His sight, and that is settled. He never takes His eyes off us as His fire frees us to embrace our true identity and trust His timing of transformation. We can and must welcome the Father's pruning and burning if we want to walk in the fullness of Christ, the fruitfulness of the Spirit, and be wrecked for God and for good. It is so worth it.

What Can I Do Right Now?

Invite the Holy Spirit to bring a fresh awareness of the Father's absolute acceptance and lavish love for you as His chosen child. Then, welcome His gentle pruning of branches in your life— those branches you already know need to go. List them on a piece of paper. Next, throw that list into an actual fire as you receive His forgiveness and fresh empowerment to live as His righteous son or daughter, in union with your holy God.

Father, I invite You to prune the unfruitful branches in my life, even though it hurts at times, so I may bear abundant fruit and reflect Your life in me. Please "wreck me" for good.

232

Conclusion

Unravel the Revelation

"I have revealed to them who you are and I will continue to make you even more real to them, so that they may experience the same endless love that you have for me, for your love will now live in them, even as I live in them!"

John 17:26 TPT

In the verse above, Jesus promises that more revelation is on its way. The mystery of Christ in us continues to unravel. We can experience more of the Father's endless love as we live in union. Such great news! But the choice is ours. We get to decide. It sometimes baffles and even annoys me that God gives us so much choice. Why doesn't He make His presence, power and will so evident in our life situations that it is impossible for us to refuse Him? Why doesn't He stand in our way and shout in our ear so we can be sure what He wants? Why?

Because He is the best Lover and will not control His beloved. Because He loves our participation, not our performance. Because He delights in our trust, not our trying harder. Because

233

He wants true transformation, not makeup on a corpse. Because He knows that apart from Him we can do nothing. And now we know that in union with Him, we can live fully human, fully alive, filled with His divine nature. It is our choice. Our Triune God—Father, Son and Spirit living in beautiful union—invites us into the divine dance.

And that, my friend, is the subject of my next book, *Dance with Me: The Exhilarating Life of Union with God*.

Notes

Chapter One: An Outright Scandal, an In-Sight Secret

1. "California Couple Finds $10M in Gold Coins Buried in Yard," NBC News, February 25, 2014, https://www.nbcnews.com/news/us-news/califor nia-couple-finds-10m-gold-coins-buried-yard-n38471.

2. Michael Parsons, "'In Christ' in Paul," *Vox Evangelica* 18 (1988): 25, https://biblicalstudies.org.uk/pdf/vox/vol18/in-christ_parsons.pdf.

3. "G3466 – mystērion," *Strong's Greek Lexicon* (KJV), Blue Letter Bible, https://www.blueletterbible.org//lang/lexicon/lexicon.cfm?Strongs=G3466 &t=KJV.

4. Charles Gore, *Believe in Christ* (London, 1921), 299; quoted by Lewis B. Smedes, *Union with Christ: A Biblical View of New Life in Jesus Christ* (Grand Rapids: Wm. B. Eerdmans-Lightning Source; 2nd edition, 2009), 140.

5. "The 2014 Christianity Today Book Awards," *Christianity Today*, December 12, 2013, https://www.christianitytoday.com/ct/2014/january-february /2014-christianity-today-book-awards.html.

6. Constantine Campbell, *Paul and Union with Christ: An Exegetical and Theological Study* (Grand Rapids: Zondervan Academic, 2012), https://www .amazon.com/Paul-Union-Christ-Exegetical-Theological/dp/0310329051.

7. Campbell, *Paul and Union with Christ*, 444.

8. With a subject so difficult, mysterious and misunderstood, I knew I needed backup—a solid, brilliant, trustworthy evangelical source—to assist me in writing a practical guide to living in union with Christ. So I turned to the work of Dr. Campbell, who taught at Trinity Evangelical Divinity School in Deerfield, Illinois, at the time.

Chapter Two: Lost for Good, Found Forever

1. Paraphrased from Matthew 23:13–34 (MSG).

2. Source: LyricFind; Songwriters: Jason Ingram / Paul Mabury / Lauren Daigle "Losing My Religion" lyrics © Essential Music Publishing, Capitol Christian Music Group.

3. See John 14:26; 16:13.

Chapter Three: Life, Not Death

1. Glenn Paauw, *Saving the Bible from Ourselves: Learning to Read and Live the Bible Well* (Downers Grove, Ill.: InterVarsity, 2016), 14.

2. Steve McVey, *Unlock Your Bible: The Key to Understanding and Applying Scriptures to Your Life* (Atlanta, GA: Grace Walk Resources, 2013), Kindle edition, 31.

3. See 1 Peter 5:14; Ephesians 6:9; Romans 3:31.

4. See Exodus 21:17.

Chapter Four: Saint Now, Sinner No More

1. Campbell, *Paul and Union with Christ*, 53.

2. Michael J. Gorman, *Participating in Christ: Explorations in Paul's Theology and Spirituality* (Grand Rapids: Baker Academic, 2019), Kindle edition, chapter 1.

3. "Were You There" (public domain, 1899), Hymnary.org, https://hymnary .org/hymn/LUYH2013/166.

4. *The Passion Translation*, trans. Brian Simmons (Savage: Broadstreet Publishing Group, LLC; 2nd edition, 2019), 407.

5. Ibid., 228.

Chapter Five: Better Drunk Than Sober

1. Paul G. Hiebert, "The Flaw of the Excluded Middle" *Missiology: An International Review* 10, issue 1 (January 1, 1982): 35-47, http://hiebe rtglobalcenter.org/blog/wp-content/uploads/2013/09/29.-1999.-The-Flaw -of-the-Excluded-Middle.pdf.

2. "H5731 – `Eden," *Strong's Hebrew Lexicon* (KJV), Blue Letter Bible, https://www.blueletterbible.org/lang/lexicon/lexicon.cfm?Strongs=H5731 &t=KJV.

3. The note for 1 Timothy 6:17 (TPT), referring to the word *need*, reads, "Or 'pleasure.'"

4. N. T. Wright, "Mind, Spirit, Soul and Body: All for One and One for All Reflections on Paul's Anthropology in his Complex Contexts," Society of Christian Philosophers: Regional Meeting, Fordham University, March 18, 2011, https://ntwrightpage.com/2016/07/12/mind-spirit-soul-and-body/.

5. Ibid.

6. Irenaeus of Lyons, AZQuotes.com, Wind and Fly LTD, https://www.azquotes.com/quote/936397.

7. Paul R. Smith, *Integral Christianity: The Spirit's Call to Evolve* (St. Paul: Paragon House, 2011), Kindle edition, chapter 8.

8. Ibid.

9. Ibid.

Chapter Six: Intimacy, Not Imitation

1. 1 Thessalonians 5:16 (GNT).

2. John 14:27 (NLT).

3. See Hebrews 11:6.

4. John 1:14. See also Hebrews 2:14: "Because God's children are human beings—made of flesh and blood—the Son also became flesh and blood" (NLT).

5. Gorman, *Participating*, 16.

6. Ibid.

7. Ibid.

8. A. B. Simpson, "Himself" (public domain), https://www.biblebelievers.com/simpson-ab_himself.html.

9. Simmons, *The Passion*, 300.

10. John Burke, *Imagine Heaven* (Grand Rapids: Baker Publishing Group, 2015) Kindle edition, 188–191.

11. Linda Kay Klein, *Pure: Inside the Evangelical Movement That Shamed a Generation of Young Women and How I Broke Free* (New York: Atria Books, 2018), Kindle edition, 7–8.

Chapter Seven: Contempt or Compassion?

1. Richard Rohr and Andreas Ebert, *The Enneagram: A Christian Perspective*, trans. Peter Heinegg (New York: Crossroad Publishing Company, 2001), 34.

2. Brandon Vogt, "Jesus in His Most Distressing Disguise," *Saints and Social Justice: A Guide to Changing the World* (Huntington, In.: Our Sunday Visitor, 2014), Kindle edition, 309–327.

3. Caryll Houselander, *A Rocking-Horse Catholic* (London: Catholic Way Publishing, 2013), Kindle edition, chapter 13.

4. Bonnie Jones, *Did You Learn To Love?: The Capstone of Bob Jones Prophetic Ministry* (White Horses Publishing: 2015), Kindle edition.

Chapter Eight: Messy Ministry

1. See 1 Corinthians 13:1–3.

2. In an email message to the author on July 15, 2020, Randy Clark wrote: The argument is that his deity would not be deity if he had not the power to work miracles. Let us accept this as true, and not only did

he remain fully God and fully man, he did his miracles from his deity as believed by the Third Council of Constantinople. What does this mean for us? If our focus is on the indwelling Christ in us, we, too, have a new nature, a new presence—that of the Holy Spirit in us. And, as the second person of the Trinity in the incarnation worked miracles, not the humanity of Jesus, so it is in us. By the power of the Trinity in us, God in us is able to work miracles through us, but it is not done in our power, might, will, strength, but in the Father's, Son's and Holy Spirit's presence that have taken up residence in us through the new birth—the new creation, the indwelling Christ in us, "the hope of glory" (Colossians 1:27). As Paul said, "For this I toil, struggling with all his energy that he powerfully works within me" (verse 29). When someone is healed through our prayers, it is not us who healed them but the God in us who healed them, His energy, which so powerfully works in us.

3. John Wimber, *Healing*, vol. 1, Healing Seminar conference notebook, Vineyard Ministries International, Anaheim, Calif., 1985, audio cassette recording.

4. Ken Blue, *Authority to Heal* (Downers Grove, Ill.: InterVarsity, 2009), Kindle edition, chapter 5.

Chapter Nine: Powerful, Not Pagan

1. Ray Moran, *Spent Matches* (Nashville: Thomas Nelson, 2015), Kindle edition, 154–55.

2. Brother Lawrence, *The Practice of the Presence of God* (Whitaker House; New Abridged ed. edition, 1982).

3. See Romans 10:17.

4. See also verses 38–41.

5. Simmons, *The Passion*, 81–82.

Chapter Ten: Bonfire or Hellfire?

1. Author unknown, "The Silversmith," Heavens Inspirations, https://www.heavensinspirations.com/silversmith.html.

2. Richard Rohr, *Falling Upward* (San Francisco: Wiley, Jossey-Bass, 2011), Kindle edition, 32–35.

When **Di Leman** is not taking long walks with her husband, Happy, or reading mounds of books, she loves to frolic in the ocean, ski down a mountain or swim in her pool with her growing gang of grandchildren. How thankful she is that Jesus revealed Himself to her as Savior, Healer and Lover for life. A graduate of the University of Illinois, Dianne left her career in education after encountering the Holy Spirit and experiencing God's miraculous healing from infertility. She entered full-time ministry with Happy, and together they planted and pastored The Vineyard Church of Central Illinois, Urbana, while raising their family of four sons and one daughter. Over the past forty years, Di has served on the Vineyard U.S.A. Executive Team, led the Women in Leadership and Renewal Teams and traveled widely, sharing God's love and healing power. She is the author of three books that reflect her passions: *We're Pregnant! How to Receive God's Cure for Infertility*, *Hello, Holy Spirit: God's Gift of Live-in Help* and *Jesus.Heals.Today: God's Prescription for a Hurting World*, co-authored with Putty Putman. Di indulges daily in Reese's Peanut Butter Cups, endless mugs of French roast black coffee and her favorite episodes of *Call the Midwife* or *House Hunters*. Jesus enjoys all of these with her.

Website: www.dianneleman.com
Facebook: https://www.facebook.com/dianneleman1/

Printed in Great Britain
by Amazon

57810721R00139